African Theatre
14

Series Editors
Martin Banham, James Gibbs,
Yvette Hutchison, Femi Osofisan
& Jane Plastow

T0339237

Reviews Editor
Martin Banham
4 Oakwood Gardens, Leeds LS2 2JE, UK

Associate Editors
Omofolabo Ajayi-Soyinka
Dept of Theatre, 1530 Naismith Dr, University of Kansas, Lawrence, KS 66045–3140, USA
Awo Mana Asiedu
School of Performing Arts, PO Box 201, University of Ghana, Legon, Ghana
David Kerr
Dept of Media Studies, Private Bag 00703, University of Botswana, Gaborone, Botswana
Amandina Lihamba
Dept of Fine & Performing Arts, PO Box 3505, University of Dar es Salaam, Tanzania
Patrick Mangeni
Head of Dept of Music, Dance & Drama, Makerere University, Kampala, Uganda
Christine Matzke
Dept of English, University of Bayreuth, 95440 Bayreuth, Germany
Olu Obafemi
Dept of English, University of Ilorin, Ilorin, Nigeria

Published titles in the series:
African Theatre in Development
African Theatre: Playwrights & Politics
African Theatre: Women
African Theatre: Southern Africa
African Theatre: Soyinka: Blackout, Blowout & Beyond
African Theatre: Youth
African Theatre 7: Companies
African Theatre 8: Diasporas
African Theatre 9: Histories 1850–1950
African Theatre 10: Media & Performance
African Theatre 11: Festivals
African Theatre 12: Shakespeare in & out of Africa
African Theatre 13: Ngũgĩ wa Thiong'o & Wole Soyinka
African Theatre 14: Contemporary Women

Forthcoming:
African Theatre 15: China, India & the Eastern World

Articles not exceeding 5,000 words should be submitted preferably as an email attachment.

Style: Preferably use UK rather than US spellings. Italicize titles of books or plays. Use single inverted commas and double for quotes within quotes. Type notes at the end of the text on a separate sheet. Do not justify the right-hand margins.

References should follow the style of this volume (Surname date: page number) in text. All references should then be listed at the end of article in full:
Surname, name, date, *title of work* (place of publication: name of publisher)
Surname, name, date, 'title of article' in surname, initial (ed./eds) title of work
(place of publication: publisher).
or Surname, name, date, 'title of article', *Journal*, vol., no: page numbers.

Reviewers should provide full bibliographic details, including extent, ISBN and price.

Copyright: Please ensure, where appropriate, that clearance has been obtained from copyright holders of material used. Illustrations may also be submitted if appropriate and if accompanied by full captions and with reproduction rights clearly indicated. It is the responsibility of the contributors to clear all permissions.

All submissions should be accompanied by a brief biographical profile. The editors cannot undertake to return material submitted and contributors are advised to keep a copy of all material sent in case of loss in transit.

Editorial address
African Theatre, c/o Jane Plastow, Workshop Theatre, School of English,
University of Leeds, Leeds LS2 9JT, UK • j.e.plastow@leeds.ac.uk

Books for review & review material to:
Professor Martin Banham, Reviews Editor, *African Theatre*,
4 Oakwood Gardens, Leeds LS2 2JE, UK
martinbanham@btinternet.com

African Theatre 14
Contemporary Women

Volume Editors
Jane Plastow & Yvette Hutchison

Guest Editor
Christine Matzke

Reviews Editor
Martin Banham

JC JAMES CURREY

James Currey
is an imprint of Boydell and Brewer Ltd
PO Box 9, Woodbridge, Suffolk IP12 3DF (GB)

and of

Boydell & Brewer Inc.
668 Mt Hope Avenue, Rochester, NY 14620-2731 (US)
www.boydellandbrewer.com
www.jamescurrey.com

The publisher has no responsibility for the continued existence or accuracy of URLs for
external or third-party internet websites referred to in this book, and does not guarantee that
any content on such websites is, or will remain, accurate or appropriate.

British Library Cataloguing in Publication Data
A catalogue record for this book is available on request from the British Library

ISBN 978-1-84701-131-2 (James Currey paper)

This publication is printed on acid free paper

Typeset in 10/11 pt MBembo by Kate Kirkwood Cumbria, UK

Contents

Notes on Contributors

Sefi Atta was born in Lagos, Nigeria. She was educated in Nigeria, England (where she qualified as a chartered accountant) and the United States (where she qualified as a CPA). Atta's recent theatre credits include *An Ordinary Legacy*, which premiered at the MUSON Festival, Lagos, in 2012; *The Naming Ceremony*, which premiered at Theatre Royal Stratford East, London, in 2012; *The Cost of Living*, which was commissioned for the Lagos Black Heritage Festival in 2011; and *Hagel auf Zamfara*, which premiered at the Theater Krefeld/Mönchengladbach, Germany, in 2011. She is also the author of the novels *Everything Good Will Come* (2005), *Swallow* (2010) and *A Bit of Difference* (2013) and a short story collection *News from Home* (2010). She received the Wole Soyinka Prize for Literature in Africa in 2006 and the Noma Award for Publishing in Africa in 2009.

Marvin Carlson is the Sidney E. Cohn Professor of Theatre, Comparative Literature and Middle Eastern Studies at the Graduate Center of the City University of New York. He has received an honorary doctorate from the University of Athens, the ATHE Career Achievement Award, the ASTR Distinguished Scholarship Award, the George Jean Nathan Award for Dramatic Criticism and the Calloway Prize for writing in theatre. He is the author of twenty-two books on theatre studies.

Nicola Cloete is a lecturer in the History of Art at the University of the Witwatersrand. She is currently completing her PhD thesis, which examines the memory politics in representations of slavery in post-Apartheid South Africa. She is the recipient of a Harvard South Africa Fellowship for 2011 where she conducted research on feminist methodologies and memory politics. Cloete's research areas include slavery in South Africa, gender studies, memory studies, cultural studies, critical race theory, visual studies and post-colonialism. Cloete currently teaches undergraduate courses in film, visual and performing arts, and postgraduate courses in postcolonial theory, feminism and visual culture.

Lebogang Disele is a lecturer at the University of Botswana. She holds a BA Degree in Film and Media Production [Radio] and a BA Honours Degree [Drama] from the University of Cape Town as well as a Master's of Arts in Dramatic Arts (MADA) from Wits University. This article is drawn from a research project which sought to interrogate and shift representations of black women in Botswana through theatre. Lebogang Disele is interested in work that explores issues of marginalization, discrimination, prejudice and oppression, especially in relation to gender.

Yvette Hutchison is a reader in the Department of Theatre and Performance Studies at the University of Warwick. Her research focuses on anglophone African theatre and history, and how narratives of memory inform individual and collective efficacy and advocacy. She is currently considering the ways in which ethnographic images and narratives of the colonial period are being renegotiated in and through contemporary performance; and exploring how a mobile application for feature phones can support a network of contemporary African women artists and researchers in exploring their work in relation to everyday lived experiences, and the development of new methodologies related to gender studies.

Susan Kiguli is a poet and academic. She is currently head of the Department of Literature at Makerere University in Uganda. Her best known volume of poetry is the award winning *The African Saga* (1998). Her work, in both English and Kiganda, has been published in many international anthologies and journals, and she has been invited to give poetry readings worldwide. She also writes academically on oral culture, poetry and song in southern and eastern Africa.

Alude Mahali is a post-doctoral fellow and research specialist in the Human and Social Development Program, Human Science Research Council, SA. She holds a PhD in Performance/Cultural Studies from the University of Cape Town, and has taught most recently at the Edna Manley College of Visual and Performing Arts in Kingston, Jamaica. She has published several book chapters on her research interests, which include identity, performing blackness and memory, language, sexuality, family and youth empowerment.

Sara Matchett is a senior lecturer in the Department of Drama at the University of Cape Town. She is the co-director of The Mothertongue Project and is also an Associate Teacher of Fitzmaurice Voicework®. Her Teaching profile centres around voice, acting, theatre-making, applied drama/theatre, and performance analysis. She is interested in integral approaches to performance making. Her area of research investigates the soma as a site for generating images for performance making, with specific focus on breath as catalyst.

Christine Matzke teaches English and African literature at the University of Bayreuth. Recent publications include chapters on *Hamlet* in Africa (2014) and a South Sudanese *Cymbeline* (2013), and she co-edited *Life is a Thriller: Investigating African Crime Fiction* (2012) (with Anja Oed). She specializes in theatre and performance in Eritrea.

Jane Plastow is Professor of African Theatre at the University of Leeds. She writes widely on African theatre and Theatre for Development, and has worked in many nations in the Horn and East of Africa. She is currently working on a book on the history of East African theatre, and on a theatre project looking at environmental concerns with the people of Walukuba, a working-class area of the town of Jinja in Uganda.

Sandra L. Richards is Professor in Residence and Director of the Liberal Arts programme at Northwestern University in Qatar. She is also Professor of African American Studies, Theater and Performance Studies at Northwestern's home campus in Evanston, IL. She specializes in African American, African, and African diaspora theatre and drama, having authored *Ancient Songs Set Ablaze: The Theatre of Femi Osofisan* and numerous articles on black dramatists. Richards is co-editor of the forthcoming *MLA Handbook of Approaches to Teaching the Plays of August Wilson*.

Vicensia Shule is a scholar at the Department of Fine and Performing Arts, University of Dar es Salaam, Tanzania. Her areas of research and consultancy include film and theatre analysis, production, distribution and exhibition in Tanzania and elsewhere in Africa. She has also worked as an independent producer/director for theatre, video, radio and television productions.

Mahlet Solomon is an assistant lecturer in the Theatre Arts Department of Addis Ababa University. She has published on the early history of Ethiopian theatre and is interested in issues of disability, women's rights and Ethiopian culture.

Ariane Zaytzeff is a theatre artist and a PhD candidate in Performance Studies at the Tisch School of the Arts, New York University. She is writing a dissertation on the role of the performing arts in the transmission and transformation of cultural memory in Rwanda.

Editors' Foreword:
Women on the Front Line

JANE PLASTOW, YVETTE HUTCHISON
& CHRISTINE MATZKE

It is thirteen years since the *African Theatre* series published its previous volume discussing the role of women in the performance cultures of the continent, where it became, and remained, the best selling volume in the series. There is an undoubted hunger amongst scholars, not only of theatre, but more widely of African culture and of African women's studies, to know more about women's contributions to the dramatic arts, and it is a hunger which the editors think remains to be satisfied. We therefore decided to produce a volume looking specifically at women working in the twenty-first century, soliciting articles from as wide a range of perspectives – and countries – as we could find.

Women's contributions remain obscured in many discussions of African theatre. While thousands of women work in the industry, and some, for example Penina Mlama and Amandina Lihamba in Tanzania, and Zulu Sofola and Tess Onwueme of Nigeria, have won national fame, relatively few have achieved an international profile. This is partly because in many places theatre is performed in local languages, uses local theatrical idioms, and speaks to local concerns, so that someone like Elizabeth Melaku (discussed below in our article on Ethiopian actresses) who is a huge national star of stage and screen in Ethiopia, is utterly unknown to the non-Amharic speaking world. However, the issue of localism is not, of course, gender specific. So the question remains: why, while at least a small number of African men have become regular subjects of scholarship, is it still extremely hard to find out about the work of contemporary African women theatre artists?

On reading the articles in this volume it is difficult to avoid the conclusion that sexist inequalities, in a range of forms, have much to do with the matter. Actress, director and playwright Dalia Basiouny discusses the huge problems she experienced from a jealous, obstructive husband in developing her career; the essential context of the intergenerational women's theatre discussed by Kiguli and Plastow was that the Ugandan government and Buganda society at domestic and state levels discriminate against women's rights; and Sefi Atta's play, *The Sentence*, explicitly discusses the predicament of an underprivileged northern Nigerian woman faced with the 'justice' of an extreme interpretation of shari'a law. It is also important to consider that many of our writers and subjects have had to contend with an internalization of the idea that as women they should not put themselves forward for 'leadership' positions. Time and again we see women 'daring', with few role models, either to use theatre to launch discussion of their position and oppression in society (see Lebosang in Botswana and Matchett and Cloete in South Africa), or simply 'daring' to take on the role of actress, director or playwright in situations where this is seen as presumptuous or improper.

As Sandra Richards states at the end of her contextualizing article on this volume, much remains to be discussed. Questions of audience reception for much of the ground-breaking work discussed below demand further exploration. She also raises the important issue of how, going forward, we should begin properly to profile and analyse the changing place of women in African theatre within theatre scholarship, both on the continent and internationally, taking into account questions of access, of specificity *versus* general points one might reasonably make, and what theorization might be relevant and useful to the field.

In our editorial discussions about framing this volume, we kept coming back to the idea of 'writing from the front line'. All the articles below are either by or about women putting themselves at some professional risk to try out ideas, roles and dreams which they see as vitally important. Some of these 'risks' are specifically related to challenging gendered inequality, while some involve engaging with broader national discourses, and some concern experimental processes and form. A number of our writers are also 'risking' writing for an international academic journal. Lebogang Disele is a new theatre maker and writer; Mahlet Solomon is a young academic; and for most of them, trying to position either their own work or that of those they write about in the contexts of theatre scholarship, African theatre, and the areas of women's and gender studies, is an experiment. We hope we are facilitating the process of raising the profile of women in African theatre today, and developing relevant scholarship for others to build on. And of course we trust you will find this volume as informative, intriguing and provocative as we have found the process of putting it together.

Postscript – In a practical attempt to create a platform through which African women artists can easily profile themselves and their work through mobile phone technology and engage in forum discussions with one another, researchers and any interested parties, Amy Jephta and Yvette Hutchison have launched the *African Women Playwrights' Network,* with which you can engage these women on the frontline at **awpn.org**.

Introduction:
Citizen & Artist
African women making theatre

SANDRA L. RICHARDS

Jalila Baccar of Tunisia once characterized herself as a 'citizen actress' (Carlson). That term could be equally extended to all the women featured in this volume of *African Theatre*, for whether working as a member of a women's troupe, a solo performer, director or playwright, these women practise art as a means of imagining a world of greater possibilities for themselves and their communities. Editors Yvette Hutchison, Christine Matzke and Jane Plastow are to be commended for presenting a wide survey of work that might otherwise have gone unnoticed because, to varying degrees, these citizen artists are focused on speaking about women's concerns first and foremost to their local communities, and are typically not included in high profile festival venues (such as Grahamstown or Edinburgh) where they might gain international press coverage and scholarly recognition. Readers will encounter: accounts of women's performance troupes in Uganda and Tanzania; a description of a mixed-gender, multi-media physical theatre production in Botswana; histories of female performers and directors in Ethiopia, Tunisia, Egypt and Rwanda; reflection on the relationship between online activism and a Cape Town performance event that drew inspiration from India; and a play about the imposition of shari'a law in northern Nigeria.

Experiences of gender-based violence, discrimination and disregard for women's lives and knowledge resonate across national and linguistic borders. Indeed, as is evident in Sara Matchett and Nicola Cloete's article on online activism, inspired in part by Eve Ensler's *Vagina Monologues* and a horrific rape and murder in India in 2012, knowledge of these experiences circulates globally. I want to suggest two large categories or umbrellas under which readers might consider the ten essays gathered here: accounts of performance-making targeted at local audiences in particular, and those that also engage large national issues but deploy an aesthetic vocabulary and linguistic register which render them more accessible to outsiders.

Susan Kiguli and Jane Plastow's report on a Ugandan intergenerational women's theatre is an example of a project targeted at local audiences. Participants capitalized on traditional skills of poetry-song creation to fashion narratives that would compellingly link women's personal and collective experiences. Unlike other Theatre for Development (TfD) projects, this one offered viewers multiple perspectives in probing, for example, tensions between being a good, family-centered Bugandan woman and having 'modern' opportunities, goods or experiences. Most important for project participants, and also for audience members, was the sharing of knowledge concerning the lives of older women, a topic more often left in respectful silence in this hierarchical society. Vincensia Shule offers an interesting account of Tanzanian women's involvement in the arts, a subject that has received virtually no scholarly attention. Founded in 2005, Binti Leo initially brought together women from the performing arts but later extended its membership to include women practitioners in all art forms. One of its most notable successes was Amandina Lihamba's production of *Nkhomanile* (2006), a play that re-writes Tanzanian history to argue for the critical role of women in the *maji maji* wars against German colonial rule. But as Shule notes in closing, because Binti Leo is a membership organization, many women struggle to pay membership fees, and the post 9/11 shift to security issues by international NGOs has adversely affected the group's advocacy abilities.

Jane Plastow and Mahlet Solomon's interviews with six Ethiopian actresses, ranging in age from twenty-five to sixty-eight, capture what appears to be an intriguing contradiction between societal constraints surrounding women performers and their love of theatre. Although Ethiopia has the longest history of state-supported theatre on the continent, women have appeared on stage only since the 1950s. Gaining training through informal clubs or in university classrooms, women face an array of hostile forces rooted in a patriarchal culture and the continuing influence of the Ethiopian Orthodox Church. While some gain public recognition, a mismatch between their celebrity status and low wages leaves them vulnerable to harassment, for example when they take public taxis home after night-time performances. Against such odds, why do these women perform? 'Respect' and 'love' are words that recur in the interviews: the respect that they earn from audiences, coupled with their love of the creativity that performance allows them.

Pleasure also explains why the women of Ingoma Nshya perform, although prior to their establishment in 2004 only men drummed in Rwanda. The group was established by playwright, director and musician Odile Gakere Katese, who as the first recipient of the League of Professional

Theatre Women's Gilder/Coigney International Theatre Award is exemplary of those women whose work speaks beyond the nation and region. Having grown up in the Democratic Republic of the Congo and then returned to Rwanda, Katese had to learn Rwandese culture as an adult, a circumstance she considers a gift, because it enables her to re-invent cultural practices with what interviewer Ariane Zaytzeff characterizes as a 'critical care and curiosity', which those who lived through the genocide seem unable to do. Interestingly, although Rwandese audiences accepted these women drummers fairly easily because of their disciplined artistry, state bureaucrats have complained that Katese is perverting Rwandese culture by inviting foreigners from other African nations to teach and collaborate.

Of all the artists featured in this issue, Lebogang Disele is the only one to involve men in her project to challenge media representations of black women. Her 2012 devised piece *Un/Skin Me* took the form of an art gallery installation in a high school's black box theatre. Much like the Ugandan women who started with their personal stories, these Botswana performers used Grotowskian techniques related to the 'heightened self' to produce a physical theatre piece that constantly shifted in response to audience members who moved through the installation. Although Disele theoretically grounds her claims about using a black box space as a multi-modal site of response (as one would expect in a master's thesis) she says nothing about whom the performance, through its mode of presentation and venue, attracted, or how audiences in fact responded.

Dalia Basiouny of Egypt offers an account that is both a personal biography of her experiences as a director, playwright and academic and a history of Egyptian theatre over the last three decades. Seeking to carve out a career as an independent artist challenging the staid offerings by state-run theatres, Basiouny found herself increasingly responding to political events around her, such that she abandoned rehearsals for a women-oriented play (*Solitaire*) to join protestors in Tahrir Square. Their stories became *Tahrir Stories*, performed first in February 2011. Later, declaring 'I am a citizen first and an artist second', she used a commission from the American Cultural Center in Cairo to create a critical piece that had to carefully navigate the government crackdown on foreign-funded NGOs. Responding to the narrowing space of freedom that the military regime permitted, Basiouny performs the Revolution's rallying cry of 'Bread! Freedom! Social Justice!' by participating in community baking projects.

Marvin Carlson presents a fascinating portrait of actress-playwright Jalila Baccar of Tunisia, who with her husband, Fahdel Jaibi, heads the private, professional company Familia, founded in 1993. Until 2001 they were largely able to confront sociopolitical issues while escaping censorship, even though theatre was the only cultural form that the government censored. But her 2006 *Khamsoun*, commissioned to celebrate the fiftieth anniversary of independence, tackled questions of religious fundamentalism, profiteering and power struggles, making her a target of the National Review Board.

As Carlson details, Baccar often found her plays heavily censored at home but applauded in Paris, Washington, DC and Tokyo, where one suspects sponsors and audiences congratulated themselves on their liberal tolerance. As with Basiouny in Egypt, uprisings in the streets had a significant impact on the crafting and reception of subsequent plays, understood as unequivocally critical of religious fundamentalism. Despite the dangerous challenges facing Tunisian society, Baccar remains resilient, enacting the hope expressed by one of her characters, who prays: 'may survival itself survive'.

Alude Mahali documents the after-images of colonialism and apartheid that continue to haunt the psyches and bodies of black South African women through her discussion of two pieces by performer-choreographer Mamela Nyamza. With *19-Born-76-Rebels*, structured for two performers, and the solo piece *Isingqala*, Nyamza relives the history of the Soweto Riots of 1976, which preceded her birth and saturate her present, raising questions about the future South Africa is fashioning for its people. From an African American perspective, Nyamza seems to be operating like a blues musician, 'fingering the jagged grain' (Byerman) and suffusing pain with a beauty that allows her to surmount the devastation that persists. However, this moving account does not examine questions about who is watching Nyamza perform, and whether these representations themselves re-inscribe pain.

In the article by Sara Matchett and Nicola Cloete, the resonance beyond Africa is both technological and theoretical. They ponder the relationship between online activism and embodied performance by analysing the media campaigns OneBillionRising and #BringBackOurGirls, on one hand, and the Cape Town performance event, *Walk: South Africa* (2013), on the other. Grounding their reflections in contemporary theorizing of political insurgencies as advancing the necessary task of challenging current cognitive maps rather than setting forth a new order, they recognize the tremendous value that such campaigns can have in producing a sustained impetus to challenge rape culture. Nonetheless, they worry that the global circulation of these online campaigns evacuates local specificity and produces a dis-embodiment that short-circuits the 're-c(s)iting' (*Hamera*) of knowledge inherent in performance. In *Walk: South Africa* (2013), a series of six performed installations through which participants moved, they see a productive synergy between online activism and embodied protest. In fact, responding to the gang-rape and murder of Anene Booysen in 2013, this Mothertongue Project performance was modelled on a similar walk that had occurred in India in response to the rape and murder of Jyoti Pandey a year earlier; newspaper accounts, emails and YouTube clips were the mechanisms whereby Sara Matchett became aware of Maya Krishna Rao's *Walk* in India. Like Disele, Cloete and Matchett offer a sophisticated discussion about audiences' theoretical relationships to on-/off-line activism but say relatively little about actual audience responses to *Walk: South Africa*, other than quoting fellow-artist Malika Ndlovu. Was Ndlovu representative of people drawn to their performance? If so, was this event an instance of artists talking to fellow artists, and is that a good or a bad thing?

Sefi Atta of Nigeria, England and the United States is the author of the play included in this volume. (Each volume in the *African Theatre* series presents a play which was previously either unpublished or published only locally in Africa.) Adapted from a monologue and published short story, *The Sentence* concerns a woman, falsely accused of adultery, who narrates her life while waiting to be stoned to death in accordance with shari'a law in a northern Nigerian town. Atta's script adds substance to the headlines often read in the West concerning fundamentalist atrocities, for she deftly insinuates the invention of tradition, as villagers are forced to comply with Koranic prescriptions of which they had previously been unaware. Further, the glamorous TV newsreader, who arrives to champion the poor village woman's cause, seems like a feminist glocal: a Nigerian national intent upon imposing a global narrative without taking the time to absorb the specifics of her subject's life.

Indeed, this TV personality might serve as a warning of the attentiveness that we, who are privileged in our education, mobility and access to resources, must exercise in receiving these accounts of African women making theatre. Luckily, there are media examples of the work of many of the women discussed here, so that we can gain some sense of what their performances look, sound and feel like. But that, of course, is only the beginning of the study needed in order to understand the significance of this work for the artists and their communities, as well as for our own positions in the global North. Undoubtedly, the research evident in this issue is hard to conduct, given the range of structural deficiencies that plague African nations. Yet, like a boorish guest who, having heartily consumed a rich meal, looks around for more, I have many more questions. Do these artists want to speak beyond their local or national communities, and if so, to what purpose? What are the circuits of funding which determine the kinds of work that get made and circulate locally, regionally or globally? How might knowledge of their work and that of other women theatre artists be expanded and brought into classrooms on the African continent itself? As an academic in the North, what are my responsibilities; how do I teach their work in a non-touristic, meaningful way? How might we all, in both the North and the South, lay claim to this identity of citizen and artist, labouring to help usher in a world of greater possibilities for more of its inhabitants?

REFERENCES

Beyerman, K. (1985) *Fingering the Jagged Grain: Tradition and Form in Recent Black Fiction* (Athens: University of Georgia Press).

Hamera, J. (2013) 'How to Do Things with Performance (Again and Again...)', *Text and Performance Quarterly*, 33.3: 202-6.

The Work of Dalia Basiouny
An artist's account

DALIA BASIOUNY

When I was growing up in Egypt I knew of no women stage directors and when I later researched the topic, I found that the first Egyptian woman to direct for the stage was the actress Fatma Roushdy in 1930, who directed seven plays in addition to performing numerous acting roles. The directorial efforts of women in the theatre were sporadic throughout most of the twentieth century, and women directors did not carve out a solid place for themselves until the 1990s (Basiouny, 2013).

I started making theatre in 1988, during my undergraduate studies in the English Department at Cairo University, in the year that the Cairo International Experimental Festival began. This festival came to rescue a stale theatre scene, which was then caught between the calcified state-run theatres living on the glories of 1960s experimentation in form and content, the bawdy commercial theatre mixing cheap laughter with tantalizing dancing, and the unoriginal, uninspired 'Popular Cultural Authority' performances.[1]

At that time college theatres were thriving in Cairo University and I tried my hand at many aspects of theatre making. I hung lights, operated primitive sound and light boards, performed small roles, bought and made props, helped to build and paint sets, created pamphlets and hung flyers. After graduation, a number of my colleagues and I formed a small theatre company and I was an assistant director on a number of plays.

I never formally studied directing. I taught myself through watching and reading. I read any book I could lay my hands on about theatre making or directing, while also attending any rehearsals and performances I could find in Cairo. I saw works by various directors. All these directors were men, and most of them screamed violently at their actors and assistants. This was not how I wanted to create theatre. I also watched a lot of 'bad theatre' and 'deadly theatre'. I was teaching myself how to do theatre by learning what *not* to do!

The Gulf War led to the cancellation of the Experimental Festival in 1991. Many young Egyptian artists soon realized that they did not need an

International Festival to perform their work; instead they founded the Free Theatre Festival. This was supported by two important women: the critics Nehad Saliha and Menha el Batrawy. A number of women were involved in the movement. I was assistant director on two productions at the First and Second Free Theatre Festivals in 1992 and 1993.

By 1993 more than eighty independent theatre groups from all over Egypt were participating in the Free Theatre Festivals. This movement soon lost momentum, but its impact was felt in the theatre scene, revitalizing Egyptian theatre and creating space for a number of women writer/directors who often formed their own companies and experimented with new forms and styles.

In 1993 I directed my first play, *The Piano*, which was adapted from an international monodrama and rewritten for four characters played by actors or The Light theatre group, our company.[2] After five years of observing, it was an exciting time to try my hand at directing, although the project faced many challenges, including lack of both rehearsal space and money for costume and props. I worked as a teacher and a translator to raise funds for the performance. Some of the cast were also problematic. The founder of the company (my husband at the time) usually directed; he performed the lead role in this production. He had difficulty in listening and responding to my direction, and quarrelled with me when I praised other actors. We rehearsed at home, and sometimes he asked me to leave the others and we had extended arguments because of my directorial comments. It was a very difficult atmosphere to work in, but somehow I managed to create a reasonable performance which was ready to present at the Third Free Theatre Movement Festival in March 1993.

The Piano was very well received by audiences and critics alike. It was chosen to represent Egypt in Morocco's Spring Festival later that year, and was performed in huge auditoria in Rabat and Casablanca. Even then I never thought it was a great production. Evaluating my own work at the time I gave it 70 per cent it was a tight production, about a serious topic, that used humour. The writing was rather didactic, and the directing straightforward, focusing mainly on authentic performances from the actors.

Partly because of the success of this performance, which put me on the map as a director, I was awarded a scholarship by the British Council to study for a Masters Degree in Theatre in the UK. Luckily, I was able to get out of the abusive marriage and travel to study. Bristol Drama Department was a buzzing place, with weekly experimental student productions and regular performances. During this time I was involved in a number of activities: directing plays by Caryl Churchill and Kim Morissey, and participating in a performance for the Zero Tolerance Campaign which opposed violence against women and children. I also worked with a local dance group, Ghawazee, as choreographer and dramaturge.

When I returned to Egypt in 1997 it was very frustrating that there was no space for me or my work. I was not interested in private theatres or the work of state-run theatres. All I needed was a space to present my theatre work. While Cairo has a large number of old buildings and historic sites, their doors were closed to me.

I started a new initiative to do theatre 'at home'. 16 million people lived in Cairo at the time, and most of them never went to the theatre. I thought: people are at home, and artists should take theatre to where the people are. My 'Home Theatre Project' debuted with a small performance in a *sabeel* (a historic water fountain) that a friend of mine had recently restored. Sabeel became the name of our group. Next we worked on *What Do You Want to Be When You Grow DOWN?* (1998), an improvisational piece about childhood and the loss of its sense of wonder. The rehearsal process was very exciting as it tapped into the childhood memories of the team, creating stories, scenes, dance and drawings. However, the performance in a downtown apartment was not as inspiring as the rehearsals. The simple aesthetics of drawing on boards on the walls, of working with shadows and makeshift lights which I controlled through a baby dimmer with my feet, were not strong enough to hold the performance together in the face of tensions between the amateur group members.

In my quest for more knowledge I had applied for PhD programmes and was accepted at a couple of universities in the United States in 1997, but I did not have the money to travel and was searching for a grant. Soon afterwards I received a Fulbright Arts Grant (which does not support academic study) and travelled to New York to research the connection between theatre and film in the period 1998-9. I got the chance to direct *Two Down the Drain* by Mohamed Salmawy at the Egyptian Arts Conference at Colombia University, and *The Person* by Alfred Farag at the Contemporary Egyptian Theatre Conference at CUNY Graduate Center. Watching theatre in New York was thrilling, from The Wooster Group to experimental off-off Broadway productions. I even experienced 'home theatre' at the established Dixon's Place that presented new works six days a week from an apartment in the Lower East Side.

At that point in my career I considered myself a feminist director, and when given a choice I would focus on works by and about women. Yet, as an eager director, I worked on whatever texts I was asked to, making sure I created dramaturgical changes to balance the position of women in these plays.

On my return to Cairo I established contact with the feminist NGO 'Women and Memory Forum', and actively participated in their writing workshops on rewriting Arab fairy tales from a gender sensitive perspective. These workshops culminated in the storytelling performance, *Her Story*, at the 100 Years of Women's Liberation Conference hosted by the Supreme Cultural Council in 1999.

I have always been concerned by how war affects women differently from men, and how women and cities are affected by war. I did not trust my abilities as a writer, so I searched for material in novels and poems. When I was asked to participate in the El Nitaq Festival in Downtown in 2000 I did not have enough material to create a full-length piece, but at the organizers' insistence I created a short performance piece exploring parallels between Arab cities and Arab women. *The Courage Just to Be* was a personalized experiential piece. Audience members entered the space one at time, and each individually undertook a journey of texture, scents, sounds, poetry and music. This piece played with the rules of performance, taking the 'contract between audience and performer' literally, asking each audience member to sign a contract agreeing to follow instructions, to be blindfolded and to keep the content of the performance confidential. It was an exciting experiment that only 35 audience members were able to experience in the time allocated during the festival.

By the advent of the third millennium the Free Theatre Movement was slowly disintegrating. Many of its leading figures found work in the cable channels that were proliferating at the time. The few remaining hardcore theatre makers were fighting for space on the one government stage that allowed independent theatre performances, Al Hanager Arts Centre.

Space was disappearing in front of me, and my search for more education led me back to New York to pursue my PhD in Theatre at the CUNY Graduate Center in 2001. I was taking a chance, as all my life's savings would only last for a few months. But I knew that if I wanted a thorough theatre education I had to return to New York, and do it the hard way.

My eight years in New York were exciting and intense, and a time of deep growth. A few months after I moved there the attacks of 9/11 took place, and as an Arab living in the United States I had to face difficult questions regarding my identity and my loyalties.

Arab American artists were galvanized after these events, and created some artistic responses to the wars on Afghanistan and Iraq. I was drawn to create work with them, to connect them with each other and help this budding group of artists. For my dissertation I chose to write about the Political Theater of Arab American Women, claiming their work as a theatre movement with its own mission and aesthetics. My position as both insider (artist) and outsider (researcher) allowed me to probe some complex issues. Most writers in Arab states are men; very few women's voices are heard. In the USA there is a clear reversal: most productions are written (and performed) by women. Was the host culture more willing to listen to women's voices than to men's? Were men getting TV and film roles (usually as terrorists) while women had to create their own roles by writing their own plays?

I returned to Egypt in 2009 to continue teaching theatre at the university, and to create more theatre work. I also had the opportunity to work as an art critic for the newspaper *Daily News Egypt*. I had to review every play I could find. It was really disappointing to attend, time after time, recycled old plays or adapted classical texts, poorly presented. My disappointment culminated when I reviewed the National Theatre

Festival about which I wrote a few articles. My final article, 'Insipidness and Misogyny in Lackluster Theater Fest', commented on the lack of women represented (only one play had been written and directed by a woman, in a festival that presented twenty-seven plays in the competition and nine on the fringe) and on the blatant misogyny in other plays. On the representation of women I commented: 'In most performances, if featured at all, the female character was restricted to being the object of desire for the male protagonist, while in some others, women were abused or tortured with no dramatic necessity' (12 July 2009).

My deep frustration with the National Theatre Festival kept churning my soul until I found myself writing a creative text that I soon realized would be a play. *Solitaire*, my first attempt as a playwright, was born out of disillusionment and the insult I felt as a woman and a theatre maker watching these plays. *Solitaire* depicted the stories of three women: a mother and her two adult daughters. I first wrote the mother's monologue, in which she reminisces about the past and all the losses she has experienced, comparing the simplicity of her early life with the magic of new technology and the ability to connect to her loved ones abroad through the internet. Then I wrote her daughters' monologues. When the younger one is stuck in traffic with her husband she faces an identity crisis as she realizes that she does not really know him, nor even herself. The elder daughter lives in New York and recounts how 9/11 has changed her, forcing her to decide who she is and what her role is in the world. She also faces the question of whether to keep or give up her Egyptian passport because of the problems she experiences at airports.

I chose to write the mother's monologue in classical Arabic, but to let the daughters speak in colloquial Egyptian, to show the differences between the generations. I planned to intercut the dialogues and weave them together as I worked on the play in rehearsal. I also decided to perform the role of the elder daughter in New York myself, as I personally carry the visceral memory of the protests and marches she talks about. I also wanted to cure my invisibility through this performance. I have worked in theatre for more than twenty years, and was a news anchor on television and radio. No one would ever associate me with the word 'shy'. But deep inside, part of me was hiding and found comfort in my backstage anonymity. I wanted to heal that part through this performance.

This project was very fortunate to receive a grant from the Arab Fund for Arts and Culture to produce *Solitaire*. I therefore could not resort to the regular excuse that relegates so many plans into 'the drawer of unfinished work'. When you get a grant you have to spend it and report on it. This meant I had to produce the play in 2010.

I started working on the design, contacted a music composer and assembled a team. Finding an actor for the role of the younger sister was easy; finding someone to play the aging mother proved more challenging. There are some amazing mature actresses but we could not afford to pay them. We started rehearsals anyway, and continued to search for an actor willing to work with our small budget.

As the rehearsals got underway, the activities for the January 25 Revolution started. No one knew how big it was going to get. We had rehearsals on 27 January and it was impossible to reach the café where I was to meet the team because of road blocks and reported riots. We moved our rehearsal to another spot, but could not focus on the text as we were apprehensive about the demonstrations planned for the following day. 28 January 2010 later became known as the Friday of Wrath. It was a memorable and painful day in Egypt: more than 1,000 people were killed in clashes with the police. The government shut down internet and mobile phone services to stop people from arranging protests, but hundreds of thousands took to the streets in defiance anyway, rebelling against the regime.

I forgot about the play. I wanted to march in protest, being filled with both fear and rebellion. I was unable to contact anyone due to the mobile phone block. I tried to find out if people in my neighbourhood would gather after the Friday prayers (the traditional time for big gatherings) to march, but no one did. A curfew was declared on the radio, so I was stuck at home, craving to participate in the demonstrations but unable to locate one. Instead I started gardening. I planted every seed I could find in the house, while listening to revolutionary songs by the famous 1970s duo, Sheikh Iman and poet Negm. This was my revolutionary contribution: planting seeds to create as much food as possible in that unseasonably warm January.

Slowly we started to get the news, through eye- and ear-witness accounts. The curfew was lifted for a few hours a day, and reinstated at 3pm to control the demonstrators' movements. Police and military police were defeated by thousands of rebels who managed to enter Tahrir Square and attack a number of police stations. There was news about prisons being opened from the inside, and of freed criminals in the streets. Many people started forming citizen patrols to protect their families and neighbourhoods.

When I managed to reach Tahrir Square a couple of days later I was overwhelmed with joy. There were so many people who were not afraid to show their dissent and voice their opposition through chants, songs, slogans, caricatures, graffiti and loud political debates. Slowly Tahrir Square attracted more and more people who had had enough. I felt that I knew everyone in the square; they were my tribe, people with similar opinions on the injustices we had experienced. I also met many old friends and some of my collaborators on the play. None of us wanted to talk about theatre; we were all consumed by the political situation and the latest government tricks to distract or appease the public. With the return of the internet a few days later many photos of the violence of 28 January were published, as were many initiatives and revolutionary ideas to amend the constitution to prevent the then president from 'bequeathing' the presidency to his son.

As I walked around the square, meeting people I knew and listening to people I didn't, I realized that there were many stories of the revolution which needed to be documented. I started to collect stories of people's experiences during the first few days of the revolution. These testimonies became the basis for the first performance to document the events of the Egyptian Revolution: I compiled the documentary theatre piece *Tahrir Stories*, which was first performed by my group, Sabeel for the Arts, on 23 February 2011.[3]

The simple ritualized performance, which ended with a recitation of the names of the martyrs identified to that date, had a powerful impact because of its rawness and immediacy. Although it premiered less than two weeks after the ousting of the president, it worked as a reminder of the events by providing detailed accounts and testimonies that mixed the personal and the political. It also demonstrated how the performers/demonstrators themselves changed through the 18 days of the revolution which altered the course of Egyptian history. These authentic first-hand accounts provided a taste of events in the Square to audience members who had not demonstrated there, while refreshing demonstrators' memories about what they had witnessed and experienced.

Solitaire

While rehearsing and performing *Tahrir Stories* I also had to prepare a section of *Solitaire*, which I had been invited to present at Kula Mihak, the Women's Monodrama Festival in Kurdistan, Iraq, Due to the difficulties of the political situation in Egypt, and the curfew, I decided to work only on the section I was to perform, the role of Mona, instead of preparing the full three-character play. This would allow me to have the performance ready by the time I had to travel to Iraq.

Working on the text as a director, it felt wrong to present an Egyptian performance discussing protests against the wars in Afghanistan and Iraq while ignoring the huge demonstrations in Egypt that had continued for two weeks, toppled the regime and ousted the president. So I started writing a new section for Mona's monologue. Although it was written 18 months after the first part of the piece, it fitted organically into the story. Only one thing was changed. Mona's original monologue ended with her succumbing to pressure by giving up her Egyptian passport, and swearing the American Oath of Allegiance. The post-revolutionary Mona decides to keep her passport and takes even more pride in her Egyptian identity.

We opened the performance in the last few days of March 2011, only six weeks after leaving Tahrir Square, believing that the revolution had succeeded in toppling the regime. The production was successful, but the audience's reactions varied. Some audience members, who had not participated in the protests, were happy to see a personal take on the revolution through the character's eyes, and her photographs and videos from the demonstrations and sit-ins. Others, who had been in Tahrir Square and experienced some of these moments themselves, were less impressed by that part and preferred the more meditative first section of the play that takes place in New York and connects the personal and the political questions.

In the following three years *Solitaire* became a voice for women in the Egyptian revolution. It toured internationally and was performed at arts festivals and in colleges from Iraq to Morocco, from Zimbabwe to the USA. Through this performance I was able to share my experiences of the revolution with audiences world-wide. *Solitaire* also made me a performer, and cured my 'invisibility'.

Magic of Borolus

My most recent play, which might be my last ever, was *Magic of Borolus*. I received a huge grant from the American Cultural Center in Cairo to produce a play about Egypt inspired by American literature. The new play was inspired by the Salem witch trials. I did not need to do any research because I knew that world so well. For years I had studied it and written about it, and I had spent a considerable amount of time with witches and wise women. With a huge grant and a great story, what could go wrong? Well, everything! Especially if your country is in the middle of a revolution, and you work with unreliable actors.

I sat down to write the text after a huge demonstration in July 2011. I had been busy organizing a march from Ramsis to Tahrir Square with a small group of friends. We photocopied hundreds of flyers that some of us pinned to our clothes, and we distributed them as we marched through the streets of Cairo. On that extremely hot summer day, walking those two miles was really taxing. I was relieved when we made our way into Tahrir Square. I set up the tent I had brought for friends to leave their food rations in, and then left the Square to look for some much needed shade. I sat on the pavement near Talaat Harb Square writing feverishly into my new notebook. People sitting next to me assumed that I was journalist reporting on what I was witnessing. When one of them approached me (half curious, half suspicious, because you never knew who to trust in those gatherings peppered by secret police) he was surprised to find me writing a list of characters for a play, with their ages, their relationships and their main motivations. I had been thinking about the play for weeks and ideas had been brewing in my head, but this was the first moment I managed to sit down, a moment of peace and creative writing snatched in the midst of the huge marches of demonstrators in Cairo.

We started auditions in October. I had not yet finished the second act, but I knew what needed to be written. Amid political activities, teaching and touring *Solitaire* in the USA and Zimbabwe, I simply had not had the time. In November all hell broke loose and we witnessed the worst confrontations between the police and protestors, in Mohamed Mahmoud Street. I am a citizen first and an artist second. Theatre work was suspended, and many cast and crew members were on the front lines of these confrontations. Luckily we lost only our voices from the tear gas bombs: many others lost their eyes, as eyes were targeted by snipers. Nearly fifty people lost their lives. After Mohamed Mahmoud Street, there was a massacre in front of the Cabinet building, where 17 youths were killed in cold blood. How can you make theatre in such circumstances? But we had a grant with deadlines, and we had to produce the play. Eventually we resumed rehearsals and picked a new opening date. We lost a few actors due to date changes, and held more auditions to replace them. The female lead role proved difficult to cast.

On 1 February 2012 there was another massacre, this time of 74 football fans after a game in Port Said. Soccer fans (the Ultras) gave security forces a continuous headache throughout the revolution. The Port Said massacre was a punishment for the Ultras and a warning to other rebellious youths.

After a few days of mourning and confusion we continued rehearsals. Some actors dropped out of the project, and I decided to work with young actresses who were students where I taught. I could rehearse with them at the University during the day and in the evening. They were taking baby steps, shyly beginning to connect with their roles and gaining confidence. The joy of watching young actors blossom was tarnished by problems caused by older actors and their egos. As we struggled to accommodate the changes in the eighteen-actor cast (including having to make new costumes and adjust measurements) our funders, The American Cultural Center, had to deal with their own crisis.

In the crazy post-revolution political atmosphere, a court ruled that NGO should receive no more foreign funding (as almost all NGOs do). Jail sentences were issued to a few people working in these NGOs, including some American citizens. The Egyptian media portrayed America as the enemy trying to destroy the country. The cultural officer supervising our project advised us to remove the American Center's logo from our publicity flyers and programmes, so that our work would not be met with hostility simply because it was US-funded.

In the final week of preparation the lead actor got cold feet and pulled out. He also convinced the lead actress that the performance would not work, and she too disappeared. We were due to open in one of Cairo's biggest theatres (thanks to the American Cultural Center's connections). We could not postpone the opening; we had to open in five days. As an independent theatre artist I had met many challenges, disappointments, failures and incomplete projects, but this was the worst situation I had ever faced. I had to find other actors, make huge cuts to the text, remove a pivotal scene of male Sufi dancers in the second act (which structurally balanced the female ritual in the first act) and rehearse with the new actors day and night. At the same time my health was failing to the extent that I would fall to the ground when I tried to stand up. The play opened on time, and the magic of theatre saved *Magic of Borolus*. It was well received, and the songs I wrote for the performance were sung by audiences afterwards.

We toured in Upper Egypt and in Alexandria, where more problems were caused by some actors.

I was relieved when the performances were over. I decided to direct my energies to other artistic forms, and wrote my first novel later that year. When I was invited to participate in the Independent Theatre Season in 2012 (an offshoot of the Free Theatre Movement) I thought it would be a great chance to stage *Magic of Borolus* as I had initially envisioned it. I auditioned again to replace some of the problematic actors and started rehearsing with new energy. It was an exciting phase of rehearsing, with a positive atmosphere; for the rest of the cast it was a reunion. Unfortunately, violence erupted again, as the newly elected Muslim Brotherhood President issued a declaration that put all authority in his hands. Society was in uproar and there were huge demonstrations; many more protestors were killed or injured. In these circumstances it was impossible to continue with rehearsals. We had to cancel the performance, and for the festival I performed my one-woman play, *Solitaire*.

It is important to do theatre about the revolution, during the revolution, but what if the revolution itself disrupts that theatre making process? My strong passion for theatre making shaped my life, and has become my life. But I am not sure how to make theatre under the current circumstances in Egypt. I also wonder whether my health can withstand another similarly rough experience. I am currently writing a film about the experience of trying to make theatre during the revolution. There are still stories worth telling.

Under the current military regime (which came to power through protests, and then immediately issued an archaic anti-protest law) the margin of freedom keeps diminishing and the explosion of self-expression connected to the revolution is being thwarted. For most Egyptians the basic rights demanded by the 2011 revolution – 'Bread! Freedom! Social Justice!' – are further away than ever. I felt the need to go back to square one and start from the beginning. My current artivist (artist-activist) activity is community baking. I started 2015 with 'Bread' experiential activities. Twenty-two years after I directed my first play I am still searching for my way as an artist and for the best medium through which to connect with the audience, even if it is submerging our hands in flour to make dough and bake bread together.

NOTES

1   There was a clear division between the state-subsidized and state-run theatres, that mostly offered the classics, and the majority of private commercial theatre that presented light comedies, written for entertainment and focused on attracting Arab tourists in the summer, who wanted laughter and belly dancers on stage. The state-run Popular Cultural Authority is responsible for the Cultural Palaces that encourage amateur theatre makers in different regions of the country.

2   I have participated in all performances by The Light theatre group since its inception. Its major success in 1992 was *Half Rebels*, an adaptation of short stories by Youssef Idris.
3   I wrote in detail about the production of this performance in Basiouny 2012.

REFERENCES

Basiouny, Dalia (12 July 2009) 'Insipidness and Misogyny in Lackluster Theater Fest', *Daily News Egypt*. http://www.masress.com/en/dailynews/108421
—— (2012) 'Performance through the Egyptian Revolution: Stories from Tahrir' in Houssami, Eyad (ed.) *Doomed By Hope: Essays on Arab Theatre* (London: Pluto Press), 42-53.
—— (2013) 'Egypt' in Fliotsos, Anne and Wendy Vierow (eds) *International Women Stage Directors* (Urbana: University of Illinois Press), 109-21.

Performativities as Activism
Addressing gender-based violence & rape culture in South Africa & beyond

SARA MATCHETT & NICOLA CLOETE

Introduction

> ... *insurgencies are passageways between worlds and therefore ways of enacting the promise of something other to come. They show us political performatives at work – activities through which one already lives what one is fighting for – and the fleeting nature of politics and the people, both of which are seen as events rather than as representations.* (Arditi, 2012:2)

This article examines the relationships between embodied performance events such as *Walk: South Africa* and online social media campaigns such as One Billion Rising and Bring Back Our Girls.[1] We argue that it is important to see these forms as instances of political performatives (Arditi 2012) in order to understand ways in which they can produce a sustainable relationship/encounter to address the issues of gender-based violence and rape culture; but that also more is needed, namely the engagement of these issues in embodied (Steiger 2007) performances, which are articulated as the labour of *again* (Hamera 2013).

Through a comparative reading of two examples, one of global activist campaigns, the other of a performance informed by global activism, the paper begins with a reading of one instance of a campaign against gender-based violence, and interrogates the use of feminist activism and performance to promote change for women in the world. This is followed by an exploration of *Walk: South Africa,* a performance event which was produced in response to the brutality of gender-based violence and rape culture in India and South Africa in 2012 and 2013. This analysis explores the ways in which performance may transform the discreet moment of activism into more sustained/sustainable mediations to promote change for women in the world. The paper argues the need to find ways of embodying the relationships between potentially dis-embodied online activism and discreet performance encounters, in order for both performance and activist approaches to continue/sustain strategies for campaigning against gender-based violence.

Arditi (2012) reflects on the political insurgencies of 2011 by focusing on the ways in which they moved beyond standard political practices or

policy-making exercises. For him, insurgencies such as the Arab Spring²
and the student revolt in Chile are about refusing to continue as before,
and about opening up possibilities that may or may not prosper. Arditi
proposes that insurgencies themselves should be read as 'the plan' in that:
'they make a difference by moving the conversation [forward], they are
political performatives [in that] – participants start to experience what they
strive to become – and vanishing mediators or passageways to something
other to come' (2012: np). Arditi's notion of insurgencies as political
performatives (2012) is useful in considering examples of global campaigns,
against gender-based violence, including the One Billion Rising and Bring
Back Our Girls campaigns, as well as reasons for reading such actions as
successful political performatives. This is based on the ways in which these
campaigns underscore the importance of disrupting the given, in terms of
both rhetoric and response to the global issue of violence against women
and girls specifically.

Central to Arditi's argument concerning insurgencies as political performatives is the need to displace our traditional understanding of insurgencies
themselves. Marshall McLuhan's *Understanding Media* contends that by
focusing on the message or content of media it is possible to miss the more
radical impact of new media, which McLuhan identifies as the fact that the
medium itself *is* the message. Building on this, Arditi argues that insurgencies
(as the plan and as the medium) are about multiplying possibilities by
challenging our political imaginaries and cognitive maps instead of proposing
or designing the new order (2012: 2). If, as Arditi reasons, insurgencies show
us political performatives at work, in that they are 'activities through which
one already lives what one is fighting for' (*ibid.*) then we can ask: what are
political performatives and how do they function to disrupt in our context?
How might we think of the global online media campaigns against gender-
based violence as evidence of these insurgent disruptions?

Arditi's definition of political performatives is based on John Austin's
speech act theory, which defines performatives as 'utterances that are
inseparable from the actions they announce', in which ritualized utterances
'require specific contexts of validity' (2012: 4). Arditi extends Austin's political
performatives to include 'actions and statements that anticipate something to
come as participants begin to experience – as they begin to live – what they
are fighting for while they fight for it' (*ibid.*) We suggest that participants in
the two global campaigns against gender-based violence cited in this paper
undergo similar experiences.

The One Billion Rising campaign

On 14 February 2012 the One Billion Rising campaign was launched
globally. Its aims were to raise awareness of violence against women, to
inspire action for justice and to promote gender equality. It began as part

of the V-Day movement, a global activist movement to end violence against women and girls[3] and was initially inspired by Eve Ensler's *Vagina Monologues*.[4] The 'billion' in the campaign's title refers to the UN statistic that one in three women will be raped or beaten in their lifetime: approximately one billion women and girls. The campaign asks participants to express their outrage at this statistic, and its implications for gender-based violence in general, by 'striking, dancing and RISING in defiance of the injustices women suffer, demanding an end at last to violence against women'.[5] Many African countries were involved in the campaign, including the Democratic Republic of Congo, the Gambia, Kenya, Nigeria, Sudan, Somalia, South Africa, Swaziland and Zimbabwe. Often cited as one of the most dangerous places in the world to be a woman, South Africa's statistics for rape and gender-based violence galvanized thousands of South Africans to rise in support of the campaign at a range of events and through various media since the campaign's inception.[6]

The global campaign relies heavily on a combination of performance activities (theatre, art and dance) and political activism. These forms of insurgencies as political performatives, in Arditi's terms, rely heavily on social media platforms to share and promote the campaign's mandates and activities. The official One Billion Rising Resource toolkit lists ways in which people can participate in activism via Facebook, Twitter and email.[7] All of the options to share, publicize, plan and RISE in the campaign are tied to participation on social media networks, thus creating an interesting tension with the campaign's focus on activist embodiment through dance. The explanation of the significance of dance in the campaign's description illustrates the extent to which corporeal embodiment plays a central role in One Billion Rising:

> Dance is one of the most powerful forces on the earth and we have only just begun to tap into where it can take us. The struggle of humanity is the struggle to return to our bodies. Through trauma, cruelty, shame, oppression, violence, rape, exclusion, the body of the human species has been hurt, wounded, and we have been forced to flee our bodies [...] Dancing allows us to come back into our bodies as individuals and groups and a world [...] It allows us to go further, to include everyone, to tap into a revolutionary and poetic energy which is inviting us to take the lid off the patriarchal container releasing more of our wisdom, our self love, our sexuality, our compassion, and fierceness. Dancing is defiance. It is joyous and raging.[8]

One Billion Rising sees a productive tension between the embodiment foregrounded by dancing and the potential of the virtual platform of online activism, despite the latter being disembodied.

The Bring Back Our Girls campaign

On 14 April 2014 Boko Haram, a militant Islamist movement in Nigeria, kidnapped 230 schoolgirls between the ages of 16 and 18 from the Chibok

Government Secondary School. With very little mainstream media coverage of the kidnapping in the week that followed, a social media campaign was launched. According to Matt Collins (2014) this followed a speech in Nigeria by Oby Ezekwesili, vice-president of the World Bank for Africa, demanding that the Nigerian government help to 'bring back our girls'. The call was echoed by tweeters in Nigeria using the #BringBackOurGirls hashtag,[9] which was used in over a million tweets worldwide. The campaign's goals were to raise awareness and pressure the Nigerian government into a response, while encouraging other governments, including that of the United States, to intervene and help rescue the kidnapped girls. A website, Facebook and Twitter pages were subsequently set up.[10] These platforms, according to their founders, are meant 'to share credible and vetted news stories, give people actions they can take and help the community around the world connect for rallies' (Mosley, Bring Back Our Girls website founder).

The Bring Back Our Girls campaign soon went viral globally, with a number of prominent individuals voicing their support. Both well known and ordinary individuals posted pictures of themselves holding up signs with messages of support and/or calls for action, with the hashtag 'Bring Back our Girls'. These images were shared widely on social media platforms and brought global attention to the plight of the kidnapped girls. It is significant that activists included their embodied photographs alongside slogans calling for political action, suggesting their wish to send, not an anonymous message, but a specific, embodied call. In the case of activists who were also celebrities, embodied photographs may also have boosted the popularity of the images and their subsequent circulation on various social media platforms.

As a platform for information and activist actions, the campaign privileged awareness of the plight of the 230 girls who were kidnapped. It also arguably put pressure on Nigerian and other governments to act against Boko Haram and rescue the girls by bringing global mainstream media and activist attention to the kidnapping, as evidenced by various official governmental responses around the world. For example, the South African government condemned the abduction and publically supported the efforts of the Nigerian government to have the girls returned safely. It also endorsed initiaves by civil society throughout South Africa in support of this campaign.[11] Public demonstrations supporting the campaign took place in cities around the world, including Johannesburg, Abuja, Washington, DC and London. In some ways less visible in the global campaign were the Nigerian activists who took to the streets and social media criticizing the Nigerian government's apparent lack of response and who urged officials to rescue the girls. At events such as 'Speak Out Saturdays' in Lagos people met and discussed issues surrounding the girls' release.[12] Interestingly, these local, embodied activities seem to have had less visible effect than the media campaigns.

Campaigns as political performatives *versus* performance as the labour of *again*

Both the One Billion Rising and Bring Back Our Girls campaigns seem to have successfully mobilized mass interest in instances of gender-based violence, and as such can be termed *insurgencies*, given the ways in which they have disrupted the status quo and drawn attention to gender-based violence. They have made the issue highly visible, even if this visibility can be seen as occurring only at discreet moments in time.

Viewing these campaigns in the light of Arditi's argument that insurgencies constitute political performatives, insofar as their very existence manifests what they call for – a global commitment to make gender-based violence visible and to end it – the campaigns can be seen as successful. However, if analysed according to Hamera's idea of performance as the labour of *again*, their success is more difficult to assess.

Judith Hamera, reflecting on the work that performance is able to do, suggests that performance is the labour of *again* in the sense that it is an act of 're-c(s)iting' insofar as it can refer to a change of location ('re-site'), and acknowledge previous turns ('re-cite') and expressions ('recite') of a performance (2013: 202). In these multiple iterations Hamera proposes that while obvious precision is important, the elements of play, including instability, also characterize both the field and the institutions in which performance and its study are located.

If performance is about 're-c(s)iting' as Hamera argues, then thinking about the relationships between online media campaigns and performance works, both responding to gender-based violence, might evocatively illustrate this labour of *again*. Both the online campaigns described above demonstrate the constant change of locations that is evoked through the range of participants and contexts; they refer to other texts that deal with similar activist work; and they express parallel sentiments about the need to promote change for women and girls in the world. This implies that participation and experiences can be read as equivalent, thereby obscuring the nuanced specifics, local situations and causes or experiences of women facing gender-based violence. This is problematic as it also implies that universal solutions can be found to the problem of gender-based violence which do not need to be sensitive either to local causes or, importantly, to the specific concerns and experiences of women.

However, the campaigns also arguably lack any ongoing, long-term commitment to the labour of *again*: the embodied action that live performance facilitates and promotes; the return, repetition and play that sees performance involved in recursive work which alters its reception and outcome in specific, although varied, locales. This is vital for activism against gender-based violence. This embodiment is discussed below in the analysis of *Walk: South Africa*.

Walk: South Africa is a performance created by a group of women artists living in Cape Town in response to Indian theatre artist Maya Krishna Rao's *Walk* (Rao, 2013). Rao crafted *Walk* as a response to the gang-rape and murder of 23-year-old Jyoti Pandey by six men on a bus in Delhi, India in December 2012. The Mothertongue Project,[13] with Rao's permission, created *Walk: South Africa* in early 2013, as a response to the gang-rape and murder of 17-year-old Anene Booysen in Bredasdorp, South Africa, on 2 February 2013. Both women were disembowelled and left for dead at the side of the road, and both died in hospital, Jyoti Pandey 13 days and Anene Booysen 6 hours after their respective ordeals.

Although there were similarities in public reaction in both countries, India's immediate civil response seemed to be of much greater magnitude than that in South Africa. Journalist Heidi Swarts notes that '[i]f the South African reaction to Booysen's rape and murder is anything to go by, water and lights still take precedence over the safety of women and children' (2013). Rebecca Davis, reporting for the *Daily Maverick*, writes that 'in India the outcry was accompanied by significant, unprecedented mass protest againt sexual violence in a way that simply failed to materialise in South Africa' (2013). We ponder whether as a nation South Africa has become numb to the high levels of violence imposed on women on a daily basis. Have we gone so far as to normalize it? Moffett claims that 'in post-apartheid, democratic South Africa, sexual violence has become a socially endorsed punitive project for maintaining patriarchal order' (2006: 129). She further notes that '[t]his is

> generally and globally true of rape, but in the case of South Africa, such activities draw on apartheid practices of control that have permeated all sectors of society' (ibid.)

In February 2013, Sara Matchett received an email from Rao, with a link to a YouTube clip of her latest performance, *Walk*.[14] In the same email Rao writes '[p]ost the gang rape there is a swell, a big swell of young people who want to find ways of expressing and performing out in the open - great opportunity for us. How and when do we meet?' (personal communication 16 February 2013). Under the umbrella of The Mothertongue Project, Matchett gathered a group of six women, postgraduate and undergraduate students from The University of Cape Town's Drama Department as well as professional performers. She showed them the footage of Rao's *Walk* and asked them to conceptualize a 10-minute performed response to both *Walk* and the challenges of gender-based violence and rape culture in South Africa. And so the process of creating *Walk: South Africa* began.

The performance is made up of a series of six performed installations, that involve the audience walking, while engaging with live and recorded performances and soundscapes. One of the installations is a comment on the phenomenon of 'corrective' rape in South Africa: the rape of lesbians in order to make them 'straight'. Siphumeze Khundayi, who conceptualized and performs the piece, is particularly interested in exploring her identity

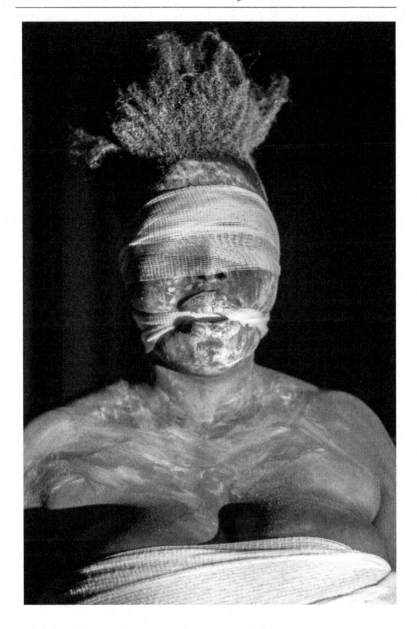

Fig 1 Siphumeze Khundayi in Walk: South Africa, Cape Town, 2014, *co-curated by Sara Matchett and Genna Gardini*
(Photo © *and by kind permission of Catherine Trollope*)

as a black African lesbian who embraces African spirituality. She views this intersection as a potential site of conflict, given the popular perception among a large number of black African men and women that homosexuality is 'unAfrican' and goes against the core principles of African spirituality. In the piece she repeats a ritual wherein she calls on her ancestors and gives thanks for their presence in her life. The piece intersects with the piece entitled 'Mother Can You Tell Me Please, Am I Safe?', inspired by a comment made to Matchett implying that white women in South Africa are unaffected by gender-based violence. Matchett wanted to reflect on this, as a middle-aged white woman living in South Africa, and particularly on the vulnerability as well as rage she feels at this seemingly imposed vulnerability, regardless of age or race. Her scholarly research delves into the relationship between breath, emotion and imagination. With this in mind she created a performance that primarily utilizes breath and vocality in its response to the gender-based violence and rape culture.

Audience member, Malika Ndlovu, in response to these two installations, writes:

> A live installation it seems. Two women's bodies, both in silhouette, both on their knees. A large blank projection screen separates them. In the dark from the right, we hear Siphumeze (Khundayi) implore the ancestors in isiXhosa first in almost inaudible muttering then feverish whispers [see cover image and p. 23]. Slowly as the lights come up Sara (Matchett) on the left, dressed only in a silk camisole, appears transfixed – a deer caught in the headlights, breathing...
>
> Siphumeze's body is smeared with white chalk paste/clay. She is also scantily dressed and soon reveals from under her clothing, reams of bandaging tightly wrapped around her breasts, unravels a bundle from her crotch, uses it to blindfold herself. This visual metaphor of raveling and unraveling bears both the nuances of lesbian women using bandages to 'mute' their physical femininity as well as wounded sites in the body being revealed to us, places of extreme vulnerability, of gendered – framed sexuality. This is intimate and intense exposure in a room full of strangers. She does not speak to us directly but she is howling to be heard.
>
> Later she has wrapped her fingers and wrists like a boxer and writhes on the floor 'fighting the demons' of memory, reliving the trauma – fiercely trying to defend herself and still pleading, praying, calling on her ancestors...
>
> Her whispers like evocation, incantation continue and crossfade with another voice as lights on her dim and Sara caught in an ever brightening spotlight breathes with conscious effort, delivers strengthening sustained notes that begin to fill the room. It is as if she is using breathe and voice to access a tightly locked room in the core of her body, a room ready to burst, a room begging to expel and express its contents. What words could capture what she articulates so viscerally – without words? An almost-melody turns into a howl, into a raging, a vocal flaming from her mouth. The smooth edges of the notes she hits start roughening, turning raw – she will not stop until she is done, until it is done. The unmuting. Tears burn my eyelids now too. What she has given us has penetrated my heart and skin. My whole body is resonating with hers. For a few moments I cannot take my eyes off her, I cannot move. By the time she begins to subside she has maintained her posture but her body seems wracked by the release. (Ndlovu 2014)

The vision for *Walk: South Africa* is centred around a sparse aesthetic that foregrounds the unavoidable physical fact of the six women performers' bodies: a fact which the collective understanding of rape culture and gender-based violence seeks to obfuscate or erase. Echoes of this sentiment are seen/felt in the call to 'dance' and its commitment to return to the body foregrounded in the One Billion Rising campaign. This points to the significance of embodiment that performance offers and the ways in which these ideas potentially inform activism.

Embodied activism

Steiger notes that: 'While globalization relies on the circulation of images and information through electronic technology, it has also been accompanied by an increased awareness of how human bodies carry out the knowledge and ideologies circulated across the globe by various media' (2007: 4). She continues to assert the urgency for performers to invest in their roles as 'public intellectuals who investigate the way human bodies perform identity, philosophy and community' (*ibid.*), placing the liveness of the performer at the heart of this investigation, where they, together with audiences, 'can explore the absolutely crucial possibilities of creating commonality while also tolerating and encouraging difference' (*ibid.*)

As evidenced in the support and appeal of the online campaigns, it would seem that this is the age of cyber activism. However, it seems all too easy to sit in the comfort of one's home and click the 'like' button on a Facebook page that has been set up to protest some or other social atrocity, or to digitally sign a petition, and feel one has fulfilled one's activist duties and responsibilities. We suggest that these formats allow individuals to disengage from, as quickly as they engage with, the issues.

By contrast, live performance as activism does not necessarily allow audiences to disengage so readily. Instead the embodiedness of the experience, we argue, creates a sustained sense of purpose and action in the world because, as Ensler suggests:

> Theatre insists that we inhabit the present tense not the virtual tense or the politically correct tense. Theatre demands that we truly be where we are. By being there together, we are able to confront the seemingly impossible, we are able to feel that which we fear might destroy us and we are educated and transformed by the act. (2007: 75)

This brings us to consider the relationship between activism and autobiography in theatre productions.

Autobiography and activism

We turn to consider how *Walk: South Africa* drew on autobiography as agency, by using personal lived experiences to reflect and comment on extreme forms of gender-based violence and rape. By so doing, we argue that it rendered the private public as a way of 'breaking the silence' and challenging the hegemony of patriarchy around gender-based violence and rape culture in South Africa.

Meehan proposes that 'autobiographical material derives from an ongoing, shifting set of relations, where individual autobiographies intersect with the wider environment to create collaborative autobiographies' (2013: 39) and that this is 'a negotiated, relational, and ongoing practice' (*ibid.*: 40). The idea of collaborative autobiographies is therefore fundamental to the idea of embodied activism that draws on autobiography as agency. The relationality of live performance that employs autobiographical material is what makes it recursive, ongoing and collaborative. Thus it enacts Hamera's notion of the labour of *again*. Embodied biographies also intersect in processes of making meaning in Garret Brown's (2013: 23) sense of inter-subjective bodies that are engaged in corporeal exchanges in the present moment. The permeability of these bodies is what facilitates the exchange. The sharing or interchange of sensations in corporeal exchanges is what inspires embodied reflection in both performers and audiences.

However, the concept of autobiography as agency does not necessarily provoke the kind of mass rally activism that comes to mind when one thinks of activist or protest action globally; rather, it inspires conversations/discussions/dialogues/debates that move people to cogitate on their role in the situation and how they are able to shift it from a point of personal reflection to personal action.

Live performance can also inspire a sense of deep reflection, perhaps what we would term embodied reflection, where the bodies of those experiencing the performance (both performers and audience) feel the need to 'do something' that hopefully will transform the situation. Here, corporeal feminist Grosz's (2008: 1-2) readings of Deleuze and Guattari's writings on the relationship between art, sensation and affect are pertinent. Grosz maintains that art 'produces sensations, affects, intensities as its mode of addressing problems, which sometimes align with and link to concepts, the object of philosophical production, which are how philosophy deals with or addresses problems'. Deleuze and Guattari maintain that '[w]hether through words, colors, sounds, or stone, art is the language of sensations' (1994: 176), and that '[s]ensation is pure contemplation, for it is through contemplation that one contracts, contemplating oneself to the extent that one contemplates the elements from which one originates' (*ibid.*: 212). Grosz elucidates that 'the arts produce and generate intensity, that which directly impacts the nervous system and intensifies sensation. Art is the art of affect more than representation' (2008: 3).

The idea of 'highlighting the autobiographical body of the performer as a site for reflecting what bodies represent and provoke' (Meehan 2013: 41) is apparent in the performance of *Walk: South Africa*. The performance does not follow a linear storyline that traces the various autobiographies of the performers involved, but rather offers responses, drawn from individual embodied histories/narratives, to the larger meta-narrative of rape culture and gender-based violence in South Africa. Meehan refers to such somatic-based autobiographical performance as a practice of 'moving away from telling one's own story [...] towards understanding how the personal is informed by contexts prior to and during personal expressions in performance' (*ibid.*: 42). The prior context of Rao's *Walk*, the high levels of gender-based violence and rape, as well as the performers' embodied personal histories/narratives, certainly provided the context prior to the actual performance of *Walk: South Africa.*

We maintain that each iteration of the performance was shaped by the varied responses of audience members as well as the varied spaces in which it was performed. This references Meehan's idea that the process of co-creating actively facilitates/includes the audience's own autobiographical experiences in a collaborative act of meaning making (*ibid.*: 38). The idea of collaborative autobiographies is fundamental to *Walk: South Africa* as performance activism that endeavours to inspire a sense of embodied reflection, or what Deleuze and Guattari (1994: 212) term 'contemplation' that will potentially lead to personal action or activism in the bodies of those who experience it.

Conclusion

An analysis of *Walk: South Africa* highlights the possibilities of live performance to add to and sustain, on a micro level, the embodied activism of large-scale macro events such as the One Billion Rising and Bring Back Our Girls campaigns. In other words, it suggests how cyber activism and embodied activism can live side by side in a synergetic relationship, where value and support effectively enhance both forms.

Although Arditi's notion of insurgencies as political performatives (2012) is useful in assessing the immediate efficacy of these online campaigns, they are limited in that they are unable to address the subsequent impact of the activism they promote in terms of sustainable action. Performance as the labour of *again*, as proposed by Hamera (2013) offers possibilities to address these limitations; we contend that this is necessary in order to promote and radically alter the nature of activism against gender-based violence and rape.

Steiger (2007) considers the urgency for performers to take on their roles as public intellectuals, experienced in the live medium of the work, where the audience and the performers investigate and provoke responses to important questions facing them in the moment. Meehan's (2013) focus on autobiography provides opportunities to consider the possibilities of agency and its collaborative nature in producing performance. A performance that draws from autoiographical experience of the performers has the potential to resonate with the autobiographies of an audience. Meehan clarifies this by referring to the role played by the audience, as witnesses, in co-creating memory in the moment with the performers. She suggests that the process of co-creating involves the audience's own autobiographical experiences (2013: 38). In this way audience and peformers collaboratively find ways to address the challenges posed by gender-based violence and rape. The notion of resonance is picked up by Grosz (1994) and by Deleuze and Guattari (1994). Grosz draws on Deleuze and Guattari's consideration of the body 'as a site for the circulation of energetic intensities' (1994: 138). Our understanding is that it is precisely these energetic intensities circulating within a body that have the ability to extend beyond the body of the performer and resonate with and permeate/affect the bodies of the audience. The liveness of this performative exchange, we argue, is what contributes to sustaining the action of online performative campaigns, and catalyses the potential for synergy between online and embodied activisms in addressing gender-based violence and rape.

NOTES

1   An excerpt of which can be be viewed at https://www.youtube.com/watch?v=SbEXlhtl_
    cU&list=UUViNfgSrQdokShK2yFuGSYw
    One Billion Rising website: http://onebillionrsing.org/. website: https://www.facebook.
    com/bringbackourgirls

2   A term used by commentators to refer to the wave of demonstrations, riots, protests and
    civil wars that began in the Arab world at the end of December 2010 and spread throughout
    the Arab League and surrounding countries.

3   V-Day is a global activist movement that aims to catalyse the promotion of creative events
    to increase awareness of, raise money for and revitalize the spirit of existing anti-violence
    organizations. It generates broader attention for the fight to end violence against women
    and girls, including rape, battery, incest, female genital mutilation (FGM) and sex slavery
    (http://www.vday.org/about#.VDvJq-cl0gk)

4   http://www.eveensler.org/plays/the-vagina-monologues/

5   http://www.onebillionrising.org/394/press-release-v-days-one-billion-rising-is-biggest-
    global-action-ever-to-end-violence-against-women-and-girls

6   See One Billion Rising South Africa: https://www.youtube.com/watch?v=VhHobzuaaXQ;
    and http://www.thoughtleader.co.za/gillianschutte/2013/02/06/one-billion-rising-south-
    africa/; and http://www.onebillionrising.org/share/south-africa/

7   https://www.facebook.com/vday, https://twitter.com/vday/

8   http://www.onebillionrising.org/about/campaign/

9   A hashtag is a word or phrase preceded by a hash sign (#), used on social media sites such
    as Twitter to identify messages on a specific topic.

10 http://bringbackourgirls.us; https://www.facebook.com/bringbackourgirls;
    https://twitter.com/rescueourgirls

11 https://www.facebook.com/bringbackourgirlssouthafrica

12 http://rhrealitycheck.org/article/2014/10/21/nigerian-bring-back-girls-activists-cele
    brating-ceasefire-deal-yet/; and http://eie.ng/ourgirls/

13 The Mothertongue Project is a South African collective of women artists, activists and
    expressive arts therapists: www.mothertongue.co.za

14 http://www.youtube.com/watch?v=msUvCWKcCVQ

REFERENCES

Arditi, B. (2012) 'Insurgencies don't have a plan – they are the plan: Political Performatives and vanishing mediators in 2011', *JOMEC Journal*, 1: 1-19.

Collins, M. (2014) '#BringBackOurGirls: the power of a social media campaign' *The Guardian*, 9 May. Available at: http://www.theguardian.com/voluntary-sector-network/2014/may/09/bringbackourgirls-power-of-social-media

Davis, R. (2013) 'Anene Booysens: Why India and SA responded differently to two brutal rapes', *Daily Maverick*, 15 November. Available at: http://www.dailymaverick.co.za/article/2013-11-15-anene-booysen-why-india-and-sa-responded-differently-to-two-brutalrapes/#.VB_3DCuSweR [22 September 2014].

Deleuze, G., & Guattari, F. (1994) *What is Philosophy?* (trans.) Hugh Tomlinson and Graham Burchell (New York: Columbia University Press).

Ensler, E. (2007) *Insecure At Last, A Political Memoir* (New York: Random House).

Garret Brown, N. (2013) 'The Inter-subjective Body' in Reeve, S. (ed.) *Body and Performance: Ways of Being a Body* (Axminster: Triarchy Press), 23-36.

Grosz, E. (1994) *Volatile Bodies: Toward a Corporeal Feminism* (Bloomington and Indianapolis: Indiana University Press).

Grosz, E. (2008) *Chaos, Territory, Art: Deleuze and the Framing of the Earth* (New York: Columbia University Press).

Hamera, J. (2013) 'How to Do Things with Performance (Again and Again...)', *Text and Performance Quarterly*, 33, 3: 202-6.

McLuhan, Marshall (1964) *Understanding Media: The Extensions of Man* (Columbus: McGraw Hill).

Meehan, E. (2013) 'The Autobiographical Body' in Reeve, S. (ed.) *Body and Performance: Ways of Being a Body* (Axminster: Triarchy Press), 37-51.

Moffett, H. (2006) '"These Women, They Force Us to Rape Them": Rape as Narrative of Social Control in Post-Apartheid South Africa', *Journal of Southern African Studies* 32, 1: 129-44.

Ndlovu, M. (2014) *Making These 16 Days Matter* [Facebook update, 26 November] https://www.facebook.com/malika.ndlovu/posts/10152855108226271:0

Rao, M. (2013) *Walk*. Available at: https://www.youtube.com/watch?v=FOZQR-TMoFc [16 February].

Rao, M. (2013) Personal communication with Sara Matchett, 16 February.

Steiger, A.L. (2007) *Actors as Embodied Public Intellectuals: Reanimating Consciousness* (Ann Arbor: Proquest Information and Learning Company).

Swarts, H. (2013) 'Will Anene Booysen's brutal rape and murder shake the nation into action?' *Mail & Guardian*, 15 February. Available at: http://mg.co.za/article/2013-02-15-00-will-anene-booysens-brutal-rape-and-murder-shake-the-nation-into-action [16 February].

Exploring Poetic Voice in the Uganda Women's Intergenerational Theatre Project

SUSAN KIGULI & JANE PLASTOW

Introduction (JP)

This project arose from a serendipitous series of encounters at the Workshop Theatre of the University of Leeds in England where, between 2000 and 2010, Alison Lloyd-Williams, Evelyn Lutwama-Rukundo and Susan Kiguli all studied for postgraduate degrees with me.[1] Both Evelyn and Susan wrote PhD theses during this time about aspects of Buganda culture in Uganda.[1] During the process of supervision I became interested in issues in Buganda society concerning theatre and the situation of women in Buganda society, which is particularly strongly patriarchal. However, since the National Resistance Government took power in 1986 and encouraged a grassroots programme of women's participation in social and political issues, a number of women, operating both alone as oral poets and within a growing matrix of nationwide amateur theatre groups, have been producing performances concerning women's issues. I was also interested to learn that the strongly hierarchical nature of Buganda society made it difficult for women to speak freely across age and educational barriers, even amongst themselves. Finally, there has been an ongoing battle since 1964, in one form or another, to enact legislation in the form of a Marriage and Divorce Bill[2] which would grant women improved rights in relation to marriage.

I had previously run a short workshop at Makerere University on Theatre for Development; Alison had worked in Ugandan schools, Evelyn had researched and practised with rural women's theatre groups and Susan taught literature at Makerere. Susan and I are practitioners as well as academics. I developed the idea that we could collaborate on a piece of work which would be innovative (I knew of no other intergenerational women's theatre project in Africa); would model collaboration with equal weight given to all participants' views; and would be a genuine experiment to see whether performance was a good way to find out about women's perspectives on their lives and a situation in which they could be encouraged to exchange

30

views across the barriers of class, age and education. Together we developed our project proposal, conducted the work, and Susan and I have written this article.

We have chosen to write as co-authors but with distinct voices in order to make clear our different perspectives on, and relationships to, the work. Mine was a co-ordinating as well as a practitioner role, coming from a perspective of relatively little experience in Uganda, but with the ability to place the work in context with many other international theatre projects that sought to empower and discuss issues of concern to participants. Susan writes primarily as a poet and researcher into Luganda music and poetry forms. (The Buganda people are the largest single ethnic group in the country of Uganda, which takes its name from them. The language they speak is Luganda.)[3] Given these varied starting points, we each reflected differently on the project, although of course we have co-written this article.

Our primary focus in this article is the significance of poetry and song in community-based theatre initiatives. Given that a love of oral poetry is widespread in many African societies, and that Theatre for Development celebrates the importance of using people's own artistic forms to promote the valuing of indigenous culture, cultural acceptance and popular enjoyment, there has been surprisingly little discussion of how groups might incorporate poetry into their theatre. This is probably because projects have seldom worked with facilitators who really understand local poetic forms. As Susan and others have discussed elsewhere, it is impossible to neatly differentiate song and poetry in many African contexts.[4] Poetry is often chanted or sung, and songs are widely seen as musically delivered poems. Oral poetry and song are major art forms among Luganda speaking people, used by both male and female poets to discuss many social and community issues. They are also utilized by a number of amateur theatre groups, including our partners, the Namukozi Theatre Group. Susan's work with Namukosi and the Makerere student group (unfortunately her academic commitments precluded her travelling to Nabiswera School) was very much an experiment. We were unsure at the planning stage whether any group currently used poetry in performance, either written or oral, and we did not know how participants would react to the suggestion that they might make up their own poems. The enthusiasm generated has encouraged me to collaborate with more poets in future work.

The Uganda Women's Intergenerational Theatre Project took place over five weeks in March–April 2010. The project, funded by the Nuffield Foundation, brought together nearly sixty women from three groups: eighteen schoolgirls aged 14-19 from Nabiswera Progressive Secondary School, a small state secondary school some 200 kilometres from Kampala; the same number of female students from the Departments of Literature and Music, Dance and Drama at Makerere University; and fifteen women aged approximately 20-70 from the community-based semi-professional Namukozi Theatre Group in the town of Mityana, around 100 kilometres from the capital. Each group worked with the facilitators for a week producing performance material from their own perspective. In the final week we all came together for four days at Makerere University where work was shown and discussed before a final programme of fifteen items, including storytelling, poetry, image and physical theatre, sketches, song and dance drama, was agreed and performed by the whole cast at the Main Hall in the University to an invited audience of some 500 people, who subsequently took part in a post show discussion.

Making poetry and song (SK)

During my previous research into oral poetry and popular song all the performances I attended in Buganda involved a variety of genres. It seems that no community performance, in Uganda at least, can be complete without a mixture of music, dance, play and poetry. For the Intergenerational Women's Theatre Project we decided to utilize each facilitator's talents as far as possible. Since I have a special interest in poetry, we would include poetry composition and performance. My unspoken assumption was that, since our Ugandan culture was essentially oral, poetry would be an easy option. This stemmed from the views I have garnered from poetry performance festivals in which I have participated, especially in Africa: that poetry lends itself easily to performance, and that it inevitably draws strongly on oral traditions.

In my workshops everyone had a go at coming up with group poems and songs. During these sessions there were interesting shared responses. Both the university students and the women of Namukozi Theatre Group explained something that they seemed to take for granted but which surprised me. The women insisted that in their practice of drama they always performed poetry, but said they had a poet attached to the group and that they viewed poetry as a specialist art. According to them, the poet composed a poem which the whole group then learned and recited in the traditional chant-like rhythm known in Luganda as *okutontoma*.[5] The idea of introducing poetry as a group activity which they could successfully carry out in the absence of their poet seemed daunting, although they agreed to try it. The Makerere University students felt similarly but were more daring and eager to try writing and reciting their own poetry.

Common issues

In the process of producing poems and songs the different groups made some interesting observations. Both the mixed-age women and university student groups noted that the process of composing a poem made them even more aware that the person or voice was key in coming up with a poem that would appeal first to the group and then to an audience. They thought that in oral poetry an involved speaker appealed to listeners. They associated effective poetry with emotion and personal experience which could appeal to a cross section of people. Both groups were aware that poetry was condensed language, and the university students tried to use the experiences gained in their formal poetry classes to write their poems and songs. The mixed-age women insisted that poetry worked well if you had a good command of language (in their case Luganda) and they relied heavily on idiom and metaphor. They used sharp, strong metaphors, although they did not name them as such. I had seen this emphasis on metaphor and imagery in my previous encounters with and research into Luganda poetry and song. In my view this approach is influenced by poetry's strongly oral nature. In the poet's attempt to make people see, hear and retain the message, metaphor becomes indispensable. As George Lakoff and Mark Turner argue:

> Metaphor is a tool so ordinary that we use it unconsciously and automatically, with so little effort that we hardly notice it. It is omnipresent: metaphor suffuses our thoughts, no matter what we are thinking about. It is accessible to everyone: as children, we automatically, as a matter of course, acquire a mastery of everyday metaphor. It is conventional: metaphor is an integral part of our ordinary everyday thought and language. And it is irreplaceable: metaphor allows us to understand ourselves and our world in ways that no other modes of thought can. (1989: ix)

Although we discussed different types of poetry during the workshops, both groups opted to compose and use what they termed dramatic poetry, which they defined as poetry which tells of dramatic moments and in so doing concentrates on the visual and aural impact of words. When asked why this form was particularly appealing, both groups answered similarly. They said that the poetry they were composing was for performance, therefore using their drama experience to speak to an audience was crucial. They also said that, since they were thinking through girls' and women's challenges, it was good to make the audience see and feel as a way of compelling them to confront those problems.

Both groups discussed the close relationship between poetry and song, and both were at first more inclined to compose songs than poems. In their discussions of song writing, the women emphasized that meaning in Luganda songs was very important. They focused on the theme of the song as an anchor for the whole procedure of song composition. They took song structure to be another important aspect, an aspect that surprised me since I had often heard it said that Luganda songs were fragmented in structure.

Strengthening community and inter-generational understanding through poetry

One of the women from Namukozi commented, as we parted after the main performance at Makerere University Hall: 'Poetry made me think a lot and it made me dig deep for creativity. I am going to tell the others in our group who were not here about it.' Guiding the women through their poem composition process was an intense experience for all of us who participated in the activity. The women presented a poem entitled *Enzivuunuko y'ebizibu* (*The Conquest of a Quagmire*). It was only generated in the final week of joint rehearsal. We found that we did not have a piece that specifically considered the life experience of older women, so we asked the most senior members of Namukozi Theatre Group to work with me to make a poem that reflected their experiences as women at different stages of their lives. The six women concerned were aged between 40 and 70.

The strategies the women used to create the poem were quite different from the methods of composition with which I am familiar. Through discussion they first decided that they wanted four stanzas reflecting different age-based experiences. They then decided what the poem would emphasize. They all agreed that the workshop had made them rediscover the significance of their experiences as older women in rural communities, as well as the importance of memory. They wanted to tell their listeners in vivid detail what their life had been like. They wanted their audience to slow down and notice the events that had shaped their lives. Everyone in the group was encouraged to tell stories about different stages of their lives in order to find the poem's content. They requested me as facilitator to take written notes and number each stage. The first stage, now translated into English, appeared roughly like this:

> Some of us stayed with our parents but hard work and suffering was very much part of the picture for the girl child. Some of us had to work very hard to look after the home. The work was overwhelming, especially for those of us who stayed with our paternal aunts[6] and other relatives or with stepmothers. We had no childhood. We had to herd cattle, dig, cook, etc. A stepmother burnt one of us with hot porridge.

When all the four stages were complete, the women transformed the notes on each stage into a stanza. They decided that, to find public resonance for their performance, they had to begin with their own stories. Their life events were key to the process of their poetry making. Challenging situations came to be viewed as poetic moments: as the images that would express their ideas and thoughts. The significance of those situations became more evident in the process of composition. In asking the women to create a poem, it seemed we had led them to review their lives and to notice their triumphs and trials.

Poetry became a process of discovering things usually kept deeply buried. It was also an opportunity for the women to distance themselves from their lived experience by blending many stories together, while simultaneously opening a window for others to begin to understand these seldom discussed lives. Asked what had most interested her while working with girls and women from different backgrounds and of different ages, one of the schoolgirls responded: 'The women have talked to us and educated us through their poems and songs'. By reconstructing their past, the group members were learning about themselves as women, evaluating and sharing their strengths, noting their weaknesses and reaching out to others. The first stanza of the poem *Enzivuunuko y'ebizibu* reads:

Mu biseera biri eby'edda eby'emabega
Bazzade nebegeyamu nti omwana
W'obuwala mumusindike ewa ssenga
Okutuuka ewa ssenga ssenga nakututunza
Wuuyo mu nimiiro wuuyo mu taale
Y'omu mu kibira ate n'efumbiro likulinze.

In the times gone by, the times of the past
Parents sat together and agreed that
The girl child should be sent to the paternal aunt.
On arrival at the paternal aunt's home, the paternal aunt works you to the bone
You are in the garden; you are herding cattle in the grassland
The same person in the forest and the kitchen would be waiting.

In translation, this stanza is a shadow of the Luganda original. However, it retains some culturally significant symbols, such as the paternal aunt. There is a sense in which the women are commenting on male power and control and also pointing to some women as extensions of this control. Choosing the figure of the aunt introduces the notion of patriarchal control more effectively than if the women had simply said that the girl child was sent to relatives. The concept of patriarchal control in this context is explicable in terms of our knowledge of fathers and paternal aunts in the Buganda cultural context. As Lakoff and Turner explain:

Basic conceptual metaphors are part of the common conceptual apparatus shared by members of a culture. They are systematic in that there is correspondence between the structure of the domain to be understood (e.g., death) and the structure of the domain in terms of which we are understanding it (e.g., departure). We usually understand them in terms of common experiences. They are largely unconscious, though attention may be drawn to them. Their operation in cognition is mostly automatic. And they are widely conventionalized in language, that is, there are a great number of words and idiomatic expressions in our language whose interpretations depend upon those conceptual metaphors. (1989: 51)

In this analysis, symbol is seen as a type of metaphor. The stanza seemed to become even more powerful in performance, as the women's expressions and gestures emphasized the images in the poem. The melding together of different experiences made the poem more widely relevant and aesthetically strong. It was a reworking of different realities into one pattern to deliver a strong message that was life-specific, born out of the Namukozi women's experiences. Furthermore this poem was fascinating because it was a tapestry of storytelling, sharp images and Luganda idioms. The poem mixed personal values with a coded performance of what it meant to these women to be their age, to come from their specific backgrounds and to have lived their particular experiences. It seemed a self-conscious acting out of identity. This process of poetry making and performance allowed us all new insights because the women's experiences became discursive references for the audience's experiences.

Working with the Makerere University students was slightly different. After the poetry workshop the students worked in smaller groups and produced two pieces: a poem in Luganda and a song in English. This was partly because students at Makerere come from all over the country, and indeed from wider East Africa, and therefore not all students are fluent in Luganda. Both pieces were strong, although the poem showed better language skills.

The students were keen to discuss what they considered relevant to them and their listeners. They argued that a song in praise of the mother figure would appeal to everyone, and was also important to them as young women. They emphasized what they termed the 'composer's voice'. They saw this as a way of drawing the listener's close attention. One of the students said that a strong voice (like an aside in drama) made the audience feel part of an intimate moment. The song the students composed, *Mother Heaven*, was popular with all the groups of participants, and also with the audience at the final performance. In discussion after the final performance, a male audience member commented that it was not only the message of the song that was positive, it was also seeing women of different ages singing as one (we included schoolgirls alongside students in the public performance of this piece) and he thought they had managed to harmonize the melody, tempo and rhythm. One of the most fascinating observations about all the performances for me was how women and girls from diverse backgrounds and with widely varied experiences bonded and formed a united front as performers and participants.

While discussing the Luganda poem *Nayiga agoba Naayiga* (*Nayiga Shuns Counsel*) the students said they wanted to involve their listeners in the poem, but at the same time they used ideas immediate to them as students and younger women. In this poem they drew a portrait of a rebellious girl, Nayiga, who fell prey to AIDS, had an unwanted pregnancy and consequently wasted her potential. The students thought that a good poem, more than any other form, should resonate with people's feelings and situations. The poem demonstrated use of intense, subtle language which had multiple layers of meaning. There was also an interesting emotional complexity, because Nayiga's past life mingled with her present and with the audience's responses. Below are two stanzas from the poem:

Nze nzijukira jjuuzi-
Ebiro mbala bibale
Twali ku mbaga e Sseeta
Nayiga namwenkanga!

Ensisi nze yankwata
N'omulanga ne ngukuba
Nayiga lino ebbuje!

Not long ago, I recall
Just a few days ago
While at a wedding in Sseeta
I was scared by Nayiga's appearance.

I was overwhelmed with shock
I even wailed
Oh poor little Nayiga!

The translation cannot fully reflect the rhetorical skill of the Luganda version. The sophisticated play on meaning in the Luganda version is fascinating given that the students composed the poem in about an hour. For example, the title plays on the tone, the morphological structure, tense, ambiguity and rhyme to give a sense of Nayiga's failure to learn what she needed to know at the appropriate time. The name Nayiga in Luganda demonstrates that the person is female and belongs to the Ngabi (Uganda Kob) clan in Buganda, but the name also carries the root word *yiga*, which means learn, and the Luganda version plays on this double meaning. The poem carries a sense of the speaker's outrage and regret at Nayiga's behaviour and failure to learn from her experiences. The students were eager to appeal to emotion and this made the subject matter of the poem immediate and real. They made a striking connection between what they thought and perceived about female education and sexuality and how that was important to the wider community.

In our project the idea of creating personal voices that could appeal to a wide audience became important and poetry was one avenue by which this aim was achieved. Poetry opened a window on women's and girls' ideas and experiences.

Personal responses from participants and audience (JP)

Unlike many Theatre for Development initiatives, the final performance by the collective of women brought together for the Uganda Intergenerational Theatre Project sought to convey neither a message nor a single perspective. Our aim was, not to prescribe, but to bring to the stage issues that the women found important in their lives, in a range of forms both indigenous and introduced, which we had engaged with, to promote discussion and interest in thinking about a cross section of contemporary Ugandan women. The fifteen pieces finally shown were those which had most resonance with the group as a whole, which presented a range of contributions from each group, and which we all enjoyed. In many cases, as with *Mother Heaven*, where other groups also felt an affinity with a particular piece, it was reworked in the final week when we all came together to enable joint participation.

Themes which emerged across the groups included the importance of education, primarily to improve women's opportunities in later life for economic agency and independence. The desire to avoid being married off too early, especially before girls had progressed as far as possible in school, was something articulated by the younger women and strongly supported by their elders. Several pieces also expressed an unresolved tension between the desire to be accepted as a good Buganda woman (Buganda culture being seen as very important to their identity especially, but not exclusively, by the older women) and the desire, often shown as incompatible with this, to engage with 'modern' opportunities to acquire a career, smart clothes and possessions, and a degree of autonomy over one's life choices. Our audience engaged vociferously with the culminating performance. *Mother Heaven* was much enjoyed and approved, while a later skit showing the students' fantasies of becoming hugely rich and driving flashy cars provoked howls of somewhat shocked laughter. In contrast, a serious piece of Boalian image theatre[7] by the schoolgirls, about how they could resist pressures to marry early, resulted in a range of thoughtful interventions by both male and female audience members. In the post-show discussion it was clear that many audience members were used to Theatre for Development productions, which sent clear messages, and some were uncomfortable with our more open-ended format which drew no simple moral conclusion.

The poetic and song forms were easily accepted and popular with our audience. Both the more 'serious' pieces, the older women's *Enzivuunuko y'ebizibu* and the students' *Nayiga agoba Naayiga*, were given quiet attention. The group recital and performance of these poems lent them considerable power and authority. *Nayiga agoba Naayiga* fitted with both other pieces in the performance about the need for girls to work hard and resist promiscuity, and with the national AIDS prevention discourse which has been a feature of Ugandan society since the early 1990s.[8]

However, in my experience, and at least according to my limited reading on the subject of Ugandan orature, *Enzivuunuko y'ebizibu* was more unusual. This seems to be borne out both by the respect for, and lack of challenge to, the piece from our audience, and by scholarship on oral poetry in Uganda, where the poet is normally seen as using a single creative voice.[9] As Susan explains above, the process of co-creating the poem revealed a series of experiences 'usually kept deeply buried': about domestic abuse from husbands and the wider family, about lives of extremely hard domestic labour, and about great resilience over whole lifetimes. Such issues are not lightly raised in Uganda, and the voices and experiences of older, minimally educated women from small towns are seldom heard in the Great Hall of East Africa's premier university. It was evident that this group of women placed considerable trust in Susan's mentorship. Their nerves were obvious as they rehearsed together prior to the Great Hall performance but they supported each other, gesturing in unison, and delivering their poem with compelling conviction.

Our project was an experiment in several senses: with intergenerational women-only theatre, with resisting the simplification of a unified 'message' through a variety of formats, and with a range of forms, among them poetry and song. One notable impact on a number of the women was the solidarity they found, by which they were sometimes surprised, across generations, educational differences and place of origin. As Elizabeth, one of our schoolgirls, told us in her final evaluation: 'I'm proud now of being a girl in school and as I move'. A major tool amongst our methodologies for producing this solidarity was the group participation, led by an expert in local poetic forms, in the creation of song and poetry which could make meaning and strike deep resonances with both poetry makers and audience members. Performance poetry, utilizing Africa's myriad complex forms of oral poetry, has enormous potential for enabling the voices of grassroots communities to be heard, but it needs investment in workshops led by experts in the specific poetic forms of particular peoples.

NOTES

1   Susan Kiguli (2004) *Oral poetry and popular song in post-apartheid South Africa and post-civil war Uganda: A comparative study of contemporary performance*, unpublished PhD thesis, University of Leeds. Evelyn Lutwama-Rukundo (2010) *Communication for Development* (Lambert Academic Publishing).

2   For the text of the draft Marriage and Divorce Bill see: http://www.parliament.go.ug/new/images/stories/bills/Marriage_Divorce_bill_2009_1.pdf (accessed 17 November 2014).

3   For comments on how it was shelved in 2013 see Rosie Hore (19 September 2013), 'I Don't: Uganda's Controversial Marriage and Divorce Bill is left on the Shelf', *Think Africa Press*: http://www.thinkafricapress.com/uganda/i-dont-controversial-marriage-and-divorce-bill-left-shelf (accessed 17 November 2014).

4   Susan Kiguli has published two volumes of poetry: *The African Saga* (1998) and the bilingual German/English collection *Zuhause treibt in der Ferne/Home Floats in a Distance* (2012), as well as contributing to many anthologies and journals.

5   See Kiguli 2004: 11-13; Simon 1991: 25-41; Ruth Finnegan 1977: 24.

6   *Okutontoma* is a poetic art in which the poet delivers a recitation with a defined rhythm usually accompanied with a tube fiddle or a bow lyre and is easily recognized by both performers and audiences of Luganda poetry.

7   The paternal aunt or *senga* is central in guiding and passing on cultural values to the next generation of the patrilineal line. A paternal aunt is also regarded as a representative of, and in some cases a deputy for, the father. In terms of maintaining the cultural and lineage values the paternal aunt would be the first person to whom parents would entrust daughters.

8   Augusto Boal (1979) developed the Theatre of the Oppressed (TO) to enable ordinary people to engage with theatre in order to challenge their oppressors and oppressions. Image theatre, where one makes sculpted images of an oppression, an ideal, and then asks audience members to come up and make intermediate images to discuss how one might move from oppression to liberation, is one aspect of TO.

9   Theatre and music have been widely recognized as forces for raising awareness of the

dangers of HIV/AIDs in Uganda, and some have credited such performances as a major tool enabling Uganda to be one of the first African nations to start reducing HIV infections. For more on this see Marion Frank 1995.
10 See Kiguli 2014: 96–104.

REFERENCES

Benstock, Shari *et al.* (2002) *A Handbook of Literary Feminisms* (Oxford: Oxford University Press).
Boal, Augusto (1979) *Theatre of the Oppressed* (London: Pluto).
Finnegan, Ruth (1977) *Oral Poetry: Its Significance and Social Context* (Cambridge: Cambridge University Press).
Frank, Marion (1995) *AIDS Education through Theatre: Case Studies from Uganda* (Bayreuth: Bayreuth African Studies).
Kiguli, S.N. (1998) *The African Saga* (Kampala: FEMRITE).
—— (2004) *Oral Poetry and Popular Song in Post-Apartheid South Africa and Post-Civil War Uganda: A comparative study of contemporary performance* unpublished thesis, University of Leeds.
—— (2012) *Zuhause treibt in der Ferne/Home Floats in a Distance* (Heidelberg: Afrika-wundenhorn).
—— (2014) 'Divine Inspiration and Healing: Oral Poetry and Music in Uganda and South Africa' in Jane Plastow and Shirley Chew (eds) *Moving Worlds. African Arts: Contemporary Forms* (Leeds: School of English).
Lakoff, George & Mark Turner (1989) *More Than Cool Reason: A Field Guide for Poetic Metaphor* (Chicago & London: University of Chicago Press).
Lutwama-Rukundo, Evelyn (2010), *Communication for Development* (Saarbrucken: Lambert Academic Publishing).
Simon, Artur (1991) 'Musical Traditions, Islam and Cultural Identity in Sudan' in Bender, Wolfgang (ed.) *Perspectives on African Music* (Bayreuth: Bayreuth African Studies), 25–41.
The Ugandan Inter-Generational Women's Participatory Theatre DVD (2010) (Kampala, Rulu Pictures).

'After Images'
Impressions of the 'after'
by South African performance-choreographer
Mamela Nyamza

ALUDE MAHALI

Introduction

The after-image is primarily produced by memory and the imagination. It is the emotional or psychological recall/re-imagining of something that is not immediately present to the senses. Both *19-Born-76-Rebels* (2013) and *Isingqala* (2011) evoke after-images in considering South Africa's past alongside its present. This chapter examines what vestiges of the past remain in Nyamza's present lived experience, and specifically, in what images does the 'after' manifest itself in Nyamza's work. *19-Born-76-Rebels* recalls the Soweto Riots and massacre of 1976, focusing on the education black children received in that era. Nyamza uses after-images of her own black girlhood to explore the persisting damage of an inadequate education.

19-Born-76-Rebels does not rely on set properties or a conventional performance space.[1] The performance primarily uses physical theatre, with very few word-based moments, to drive the plot. The focus is on the actor's ornate and telling costumes and their physicality and interaction with each other in the space. In performance, each scene is designated a separate playing space; first there is the introduction of two polarizing figures standing (on makeshift stilts) opposite one another centre stage. Their ten minute standoff includes only slight movements as they simultaneously look down, signalling the distance to the ground. Neither figure wants to make the first move; one lifts her arms as if to take a step, but then does not. This play is mirrored and repeated between them. The performers then disrobe and transition into young girls in the next scene, upstage on a stairway, at first cheerful as they run and play. The German shepherd dogs, visible from the margins, form part of the action, reminding the girls and audience mnemonically about colonial power, signalled through these guard animals. The mood quickly turns sober as the girls are intimidated in the next scene, which takes place downstage centre, and in the following scenes. This sets the tone for the rest of the performance, which is dominated by a huge book (the only set property) in a make-believe schoolroom. The physical interaction with the book in the imagined schoolroom highlights how these girls experienced school as an ordeal, a burden, and evokes the inequality of their education which leaves them exhausted, sweating and breathless as they eventually walk off stage slowly, carrying the book. The audience is involved in the action, not because the performers interact with them directly, but because there is no real sense of where the playing space begins and ends.

Isingqala is a solo work exploring the intersections between Nyamza and her past, and the way in which she juxtaposes a traumatized country with her own devastating past: Nyamza's mother was 'raped and strangled to death' (Nyamza 2014). *Isingqala* is also primarily physical theatre, without word-based moments.[2] The performance space in *Isingqala* is bare except for a coffin-like box hanging from the ceiling. For the most part, the performance takes place in darkness, and when the audience enters they are greeted by Nyamza's harrowing screams as they look for their seats. From then on, nothing is heard except Nyamza's feet as they hit the ground, and all we see of her is a series of glimpses where the minimal light, provided by erratically roving handheld torches, permits. She runs in a circle for six minutes. She stops with her back to the audience and gesticulates for some time; her corporeal virtuosity is unmistakable here as she seems to combine fighting off an attacker, making love and praying emphatically. The whole time we hear nothing except for occasional screams, heavy breathing and sporadic sobbing. She lifts her arm up and down repetitively and violently as if to strike, but instead, every time she lowers her arm, she drops a white spinning top that gyrates in silence as the audience watches and listens.

Both *19-Born-76-Rebels* and *Isingqala* have been performed in non-traditional venues transformed into theatrical spaces: for example, a gallery, a hall and in a city square. The audience usually sits, in no particular order, surrounding the action. *19-Born-76-Rebels* can run for anywhere between 15 and 45 minutes, and *Isingqala* between 15 and 30 minutes. The action has evolved over the years depending on where and for whom each production is performed. Rather than depending on linear narratives or set properties, the performances use repeated physical imagery to tell a story.

19-Born-76-Rebels and *Isingqala* can be considered both as criticisms of a disappointing present, and as celebrations of survival, in that they incorporate stories about surviving personal and historical trauma. The 'beautiful pain syndrome' characterizes Nyamza's work: no matter how painful the subject is, she explores it; she draws it nearer to herself because these experiences reveal something about her that she finds too poignant to overlook. Thus, Nyamza intricately weaves beauty and aesthetic form into narratives of pain, loss and change for ameliorative purposes. This does not mean that the concept of survival is not problematized: Nyamza's work acknowledges on one hand a social, political and economic inertia in South Africa, and on the other hand progress, in that women like herself have been afforded opportunities that were not possible in the past, even while she highlights a need for greater transformation. Unsurprisingly, Nyamza's work is woman-centred: she points out 'as a child who grew up in Gugulethu, as a black woman, there are so many challenges […] even to get to where I am today' (cited in Youngblood 2013).

In *Isingqala*, an isiXhosa word meaning 'sorrow', typically characterized by incessant weeping, Nyamza is suggesting that the whole country is still in profound mourning, but also that the state of womanhood, particularly that which exists outside of heteronormative practice, is in a state of *isingqala*.

An openly homosexual Xhosa woman in her late thirties, Nyamza has created mostly physical and non-text-based performances, but recently she has begun experimenting with vocal performance and text. As a trained ballet dancer she uses her body as text and personal experience to investigate topics such as domesticity, sexual violence, sexuality, custom, motherhood and the commodification of the black female body (Samuel 2011: 44). In the last six years Nyamza has created some ten original productions and has become influential in the South African theatre-making and performance world, critiquing philosophies on the ideal female form reinforced by the ballet aesthetic, as well as exploring shifting perspectives on female identities, formed from a patriarchal social perspective in her performances.

In the same way that social norms which favour men are uniformly part of socialization, black woman theatre makers like Nyamza are establishing new standards, new ways of being that depict the multifaceted identities that constitute black womanhood. Thérèse Migraine-George in *African Women and Representation: From performance to politics* (2008) draws attention to the African woman playwright and performer and her role in particularizing multidimensional and dynamic forms of representation to discover the spaces from which African women can speak and have spoken (Migraine-George 2008: 8). The African woman theatre maker not only has to reflect on representation and address the content of that representation, but must also maintain awareness of the processes and politics of representation by questioning blind spots, discontinuities, gaps and silences (*ibid.*) Nyamza's sentient body serves as a tool for expression of this largely hitherto suppressed discourse. Jeanie Forte observes, 'one crucial aspect of contemporary feminism is the expression of pain, the pain of the female body in patriarchal culture' (1992: 252).

While this chapter is primarily about after-images in Nyamza's *19-Born-76-Rebels* and *Isingqala*, South Africa's troubled historical legacy is an unavoidably integral part of the exploration. The painful effects of apartheid and its aftermath continue to devastate the social fabric of South Africa and, as a result, ambiguous patterns of the telling of pain have emerged. Anne Coombes in *History After Apartheid: Visual Culture and Public Memory in a Democratic South Africa*, deliberates the consequences that South Africa's dual legacies of colonialism and apartheid have had on the present (2003: 4) suggesting that the gross violation of the human rights of 'non-white' persons under the law of apartheid is irreparable. One of the statutes most damaging to the progress of black South Africans was the Bantu Education Act: Act No. 47 of 1953. This created a black Education Department under the Department of Native Affairs that established a curriculum which met what Hendrik Verwoerd, then Minister of Native Affairs and later Prime Minister, described as the character, class and needs of black people (Stent 1994: 60). In other words, this legislation legally prevented non-white Africans from receiving an education that would empower them for skilled work and professional positions, predetermining their futures by equipping them only with skills to serve other black people in the homelands, or to work as labourers for white South Africans.

The title *19-Born-76-Rebels* cites the Soweto uprisings of 16 June 1976, when black schoolchildren protested against overcrowded classrooms, ill-equipped teachers, and the imposition of Afrikaans as the compulsory language of instruction (Pohlandt-McCormick 2000: 23). In a scene in *19-Born-76-Rebels*, the schoolgirls (played by Nyamza and Magnet Theatre's Faniswa Yisa[3]) open a large book and reveal in large print, for the audience to see, the annual budget for education assigned to each racial group. The money assigned to black education is meagre compared to that assigned to whites, and the size of the printed font in the book corresponds with the varying figures. These schoolchildren were fighting against a political ideology that had little regard for how language and its absence – silence – constituted a form of physical and discursive violence (*ibid.*) This is typified in *19-Born-76-Rebels* when Nyamza and Yisa, in a sometimes absurdly comical exercise, routinely regurgitate the Afrikaans they have been taught and diligently repeat words: aware of their economic and educational inequality, but undeterred in their desire to learn, despite frequent beatings for mispronouncing words. They hold their hands out, anticipating the violence and count each lash in Afrikaans, '*een, twee, drie, vier*' ('one, two, three, four'). They repeat this sequence in a rhythmic gestural fashion, holding their hands out in front of them, then behind their heads, behind their backs, until their voices fade in exhaustion, and they simultaneously lower their bodies to the ground to rest. In a similar exercise, the two hold the large brown paper-covered book up across their bodies while standing behind one another. They receive more beatings, smacking their respective hands on the book, and with each smack they flinch with pain. This emphasis on corporal punishment highlights how desperately these children wanted an education in order to rise above their circumstances. The political and conceptual tyrannies are shown working together to keep them oppressed through aggressive methods of pedagogic discipline, where even school became an unsafe space for a black child.

Although the uprisings belong to the past, the event and its surrounding circumstances have left after-images wrought with pain, anger, distrust and questions, including what did those schoolchildren fight for, are many still fighting, and if so why? Perhaps we have not learnt from history: this is what Nyamza argues when she asserts: 'I have found when creating work that deals with politics, white South Africans say, "Oh no, let's leave the past behind". But as artists, we bring a different context [to the subject]. In *19-Born-76-Rebels*, I say we are repeating what we were fighting against. I would like to see how a broader audience would react to this piece if I showed it locally' (cited in Kamaldien 2013).

Nyamza is iterating that the prejudice and discrimination stimulated and sanctioned by apartheid have been internalized by most, to some degree (Coombes 2003: 3). A combination of these historical conditions and their political and social legacies have made the transition to democracy from the late 1980s to the present tumultuous and still problematic (*ibid.*: 7).

1976 is the year in which Mamela Nyamza and her co-performer in *19-Born-76-Rebels*, Faniswa Yisa, were born. They personify the beauty of new life emerging in the midst of painful and ugly circumstances, of riotous mass killings and security crackdowns. Both were raised in Gugulethu Township just outside Cape Town, and attended Fezeka High School together. Nyamza and Yisa work around the theme of 1976 to interrogate how this period of political and social upheaval resonates in contemporary South Africa. Nyamza recounts a story, told to her by her mother, about running away from riot police in Gugulethu and being peppered with buckshot while heavily pregnant in 1976. Nyamza reflected on this story in a show talkback: 'so, we survived these protests, we experienced it all in our mothers' wombs ... so what do we say about it? We are born from that, so where to now? Coming out of it, what do we do with it?' (Nyamza 2013b). Later, after the show's July debut at the Festival d'Avignon, France, she mused: 'the laws have changed but the reality has not changed,' as she remarks that her child is still being taught Afrikaans as part of the school curriculum (Masango & Selander 2013). In the second decade of this new millennium we are still having conversations similar to those we were having at the start of democracy some twenty years ago.[4] Nyamza adds that that we are still a country and a people in pain (*ibid.*) Contemporaneity demands that we look at the past as well as at what has not happened yet, and what is currently happening (Nuttal 2004: 731): this is in effect the 'after'.

In *The Body in Pain: The making and unmaking of the world* (1985) and *On Beauty and Being Just* (1999) Elaine Scarry affirms beauty's existence, reminding us that beauty is real, legitimate and a fundamental part of our way of life, despite its conceptual authenticity sometimes being challenged.[5] Scarry goes on to maintain that beauty and pain are attached to the body in a way that is undeniable because they are both experienced and expressed through the body. This idea is integral to Nyamza's performance as she moves with poignancy and disquieting beauty. For example when she viscerally recalls and physically enacts the corporal punishment that she experienced and came to expect, she expresses lived experience and an aestheticized representation of abuse. Nyamza's movement is also beautiful because of her precision in performance. Scarry's political critique on beauty suggests that in such contexts aesthetic beauty may be problematic because by consuming our attention beauty can distract awareness from immoral social actions and make us inattentive to injustice (1999: 58). However, Scarry also argues that while beauty distracts us from suffering it can also help to tackle injustice by requiring an audience to immerse itself in acts of seeing and hearing so that they cannot remain uncaring (*ibid.*: 62).

In Nyamza's work, pain and beauty *do things*. Pain is the driver of the material under consideration, and beauty is the performance vehicle. Here, performance relies on the ability of beautiful symbolic arrangements to materialize experiences that can be described in relation to painful sentiments. Pain is both a consequence and, at the same time, a motivation: a consequence of *becoming aware*, and a motivation for actively engaging with a troubled history and fractured identity. The beautification of pain is a meaning-making tool. In other words, beauty is intermediary because beauty can be found in and through works of pain, since it is the art-maker who 'carves pain into the ears of the uncaring and converts the rustiness of pain into the ripeness of rebirth for society' (Launko 2000: viii).

In production

Nyamza utilizes and incorporates familiar, iconic, visually beautiful and striking after-images. These are the material and visual prompts that cite memory and rouse imaginative feelings of the immediacy of the past's effects on the present. At first the after-image is exemplified in the arresting costumes worn by Nyamza and Yisa, which anticipate the political undertones of the work. Standing erect with unwavering assurance, dressed in an orange and blue skirt, with a ruffled white blouse peeking out from under her bright orange jacket, and a Union Jack bow tie, Nyamza epitomizes colonial rule. Her costume references the colours of the old South African and British flags and thereby evokes imperial histories as she stares down at onlookers with a sense of superiority. Yisa, in contrast, is dressed in green and black, with a voluminous yellow skirt completing her outfit. This references the colours of the African National Congress (ANC) as well as three of the six colours of the new South African flag. This deliberate costuming represents opposite ends of the political spectrum: British occupation and later Afrikaner rule, and the black freedom fighters and democratic political leaders. Later, they both reveal that they are wearing underwear with the old national flag emblazoned across their backsides, thus suggesting that, regardless of the surface reconciliation, the after-image and scars of apartheid are hidden things that we wear daily.

Immediately noticeable is that both Nyamza and Yisa are elevated on empty coffee tins that function as makeshift stilts. Walking on these tins is risky and difficult, the pair stumble and shuffle uncertainly: care and negotiation are required, reflecting how they experience South Africa's transition into democracy. Negotiation plays out in *19-Born-76-Rebels* through an intense ten-minute interaction between Nyamza and Yisa involving very little physical movement. While Nyamza poses regally between deliberately slow and considered curtseying movements, Yisa, in close proximity, circles Nyamza while staring her down: Nyamza's imperiousness meets a frank challenge in Yisa's upturned chin.

The confrontation reads like a dance as the pair raise and lower their arms simultaneously, gazing thoughtfully at the ground, aware that the stilts pose the constant risk of an awkward fall. During the confrontation Nyamza has a tape recorder hidden in her costume, and from her person we hear the voice of Mamphela Ramphele, anti-apartheid activist, medical doctor, anthropologist and author, voicing her thoughts on the state of the nation; what she considers to be the failings of the Truth and Reconciliation Commission (TRC),[6] education policy and the dangers of Bantu education and its disservice to black people. A formidable force, Ramphele was the first black female Vice-Chancellor of the University of Cape Town, and the first black female Managing Director of the World Bank. Ramphele, whose platform is education, acknowledges the revolt led by young people against the poor quality of education in 1976 as she speaks of the still shocking conditions of most South African education in the twenty-first century. She too asks whether the youth of 1976 fought in vain.[7] Ramphele aspired to more than was on offer to her as a young girl: she grew up wanting to be a doctor. Nyamza wanted to be a dancer, but both were led to believe that such aspirations were unrealistic and impossible.[8] However, they have both risen above the expectations and limitations prescribed for them.

Nyamza and Yisa, physically embodying the merging of the two parties, walk together and ascend a staircase set to the back of the stage. When they reach the top they join hands and raise them high, recalling the image of Nelson Mandela and F.W. De Klerk standing together in front of the Union Building after the first presidential inauguration on 10 May 1994, unified as they addressed a new South Africa full of hope and possibility. The emphasis on this moment of hopeful reconciliation in the work highlights the failures and the promises that have yet to be fulfilled. This is emphasized in what follows: Nyamza and Yisa discard their elaborate costumes, revealing typical South African school uniforms, as they revert to playing schoolgirls. There are two German shepherd dogs on the sidelines, referencing apartheid police dogs generally, but also Nyamza's personal experience of police and dogs patrolling her school, particularly during periods of political unrest. The girls, intidimated, back away from the dogs slowly, kneeling one leg at a time. This gives a corporeal sense of the fear and intimidation experienced by black South Africans every day under apartheid, and which remains as an after-effect in peoples' responses to dogs.

The performers transition to the next scene singing the Xhosa hymn, *lizalise idinga lakho* (*The forgiveness of sins makes a person whole*) which was sung as a morning prayer in their school, and at the TRC, and walk down a brown paper path, to a large school workbook covered in the same brown paper. Nyamza and Yisa repeat gestures indicating enduring corporal punishment and the ritual of morning prayers at school, and then with deep fear and dread, wringing their hands nervously and looking at each other, they simultaneously reach to turn over the pages of the oversized book. It is clear that education is daunting, rather than a nurturing opportunity where questioning and personal growth are encouraged. Instead, school elicited fear which was disempowering. The girls sit side by side with the book open across their laps, scratching the pages in an up and down motion that reflects the violence that the education system has enacted upon them by ignoring their language and personal needs. Their scratching becomes feverish, as though they are trying to erase or even unlearn what they have been taught. They are overcome by the size and weight of the book and topple over. Yisa lodges the book between her teeth, Nyamza cloaks herself in the brown paper, and they walk out, carrying together the burden of this fragmented, inadequate and meagre education out of the venue. The show not only makes visible the after-effects of this education system on these women, but also celebrates their surviving it: Nyamza triumphantly declared in a show talk-back '[even] with that education, I'm here today' (Nyamza 2013b); and Yisa echoed: 'what we are celebrating about the harsh reality of how we grew up is the fact that we survived it' (Youngblood 2013).

Although Nyamza chooses to refer to Ramphele's criticism of the TRC, it is important not to under-estimate its contribution to contemporary South Africa. Heidi Grunebaum in *Memorializing the Past* (2011) reflects on the effects of time and historicity, which have shaped what it means to live with and understand brutality and pain in South Africa in the wake of the TRC.[9] She argues that it was through the TRC process that a public language of 'memory' materialized, which in turn has informed collective approaches to meaning-making about and after apartheid, which we still use to find ways of making meaning now (*ibid*.: 2). It is notable that 'after' alludes to both a past and a later time, to what is 'behind' and what 'follows', and so it is both retrospective and forward-looking. The problems captured by the 'beautiful pain syndrome' in *19-Born-76-Rebels* are directly catalysed by the wounds of apartheid with which the TRC started to engage in the 1990s. The ability for pain to draw individuals in was seen in the extraordinary public performances of pain produced by South Africa's history by way of the TRC, which looked explicitly at black pain in a way that had not been done before, particularly by rendering black pain, which had not been visible, visible. Thus the TRC is a useful antecedent in elucidating after-images.

Black American theorist Carol Henderson, writing about the scarring of the black body, defines scarring as: 'a mark left on the skin or other tissue after a wound, burn, ulcer, pustule, lesion has healed, a marring or disfiguring mark on anything, the lasting mental or emotional effects of suffering or anguish' (2002: 3). Thus our corporeality tells its own story, and this is becoming more apparent in South African contemporary performance, in which the black body carries the scars of both a reluctantly inherited history and a present spent trying to repair the many wrongs of the past. Henderson's notion of scarring is reiterated by Nyamza who is aware of her position as an inheritor of a shameful and painful past. The 1976 new-borns were products of a period of violence, resistance, rebellion, protest and political activism. Nyamza writes:

> Those in the wombs of their mothers at the time still carry the scars and wounds of those times of suffering today - if not in a real, then definitely in a symbolic manner; [the] mother's feelings, emotions, pains, trials and tribulations, rebelliousness, fighting the good fight as it were, having been transferred from mother to child-in-the-womb through the (symbolic/abstract) umbilical cord. Today's adult of 1976 is reliving and reinventing those womb experiences of then and like mother needs to continue to fight the good fight. (2013a)

'The cry' as a vocal after-image

> 'It was a sound that broke the back of words'
> Toni Morrison 1997: 261

Shedding tears is perhaps the most recognizable way of corporeally and vocally expressing pain. In *19-Born-76-Rebels* and *Isingqala* crying, and crying out, are the most frequently repeated aesthetic expressions of pain. Despite their best attempts at Afrikaans, the black girls in *19-Born-76-Rebels* are repeatedly beaten and cry out in pain. However, crying also serves as a metaphor for the effect of the performance on its witnesses. The cry/crying reverberates, it is at once distant and close by, be it in the piercing cry of the performers or their pained looks.

This recalls an iconic moment during the TRC when, during Nomonde Calata's testimony as the wife of slain activist Fort Calata, she broke into a loud wail (Cole 2010: 11). Cole argues that this wail captured something fundamental about the experience of gross violations of human rights and signalled the extent to which visceral and vocal expression was vital to the TRC process (*ibid.*, 11). This expression of pain was complex because Calata's cry was both personal and suggestive of the pain of a whole nation over many generations. Enclosed in that wail was the complicity of citizens, the admonishment of perpetrators, as well as grief and shame and an allegation against an evil system. The TRC transcripts did not annotate or translate the non-verbal expressions of pain (such as 'cries', 'screams', 'sighs' or 'moans'). This is where art has intervened and extended the process. *19-Born-76-Rebels* and *Isingqala* pay close attention to non-verbal dimensions in an exploratory and structured manner.

Nyamza works even more deliberately with non-verbal expression of pain in *Isingqala*. Here 'the cry' encapsulates truthful and actual crying, artificial staged crying, crying out, the imagery that permeates the cry and the socio-political history of the gravity and profundity of the cry's origin.

The cry signifies the conversion of pain and suffering into a social and artistic vessel, an imaginative medium. Loosely translated from isiXhosa into English, the word *isingqala* describes the moment when one has been crying so hard that the tears and wailing necessarily subside, leaving one catching one's breath between barely audible whimpers. Nyamza writes:

> Let me begin with the bigger picture - the country as a whole. I think we are in a state of *isingqala*, we are crying inside. This is a kind of 'aftermath'. In fact, we seem to be in a constant state of 'aftermath' or 'recovery'. This crying does not end, the sounds seem different but I feel they are for the same things, about the same things. We seem to say the same things, ask for the same things; we seem to cry for the same things and yet we seem not to understand one another. I wonder what happens when that quiet crying inside becomes sound, what happens when that 'private' becomes 'public'? When others find their own cries in you? I would say that this is the human condition of continuation as a cry. (2012)

Apart from a single dim lightbulb, the only lighting in *Isingqala* is provided by handheld torches: when these are not focused Nyamza is in complete darkness. No soundtrack or audio is used. In this intimate and inward looking work, Nyamza's back is, for the most part, to the audience. The work begins in utter darkness, with a primal scream. Nyamza, dressed in a shiny grey man's suit, white shirt and tie, and black shoes, circles the perimeter of the stage repeatedly and monotonously. At first she runs slowly and then, gaining momentum as she runs, she screams. The scream reverberates; it is a scream of fear, as of someone running from danger. The scream evolves into something that sounds like an ambulance or a police siren. She continues to run in a circle for some time. When she quietens down, we hear her breathing and whimpering. The space is delineated by rocks in the shape of a square which she runs around. A flashlight follows her so that we occasionally catch a glimpse of her running feet and body. Nyamza slows to a brisk shuffle, then a march, and her circle begins to narrow. She removes the jacket and uses it to hide her face as she continues her shuffling march.

The scream sets the tone for *Isingqala*, and in the moments that follow Nyamza's body casts a shadow against the wall. With her back to the audience she violently and sporadically flails her arms and body. She cries uncontrollably, her chest and shoulders frenetically heaving up and down as she sobs. The heaving movement in her upper body becomes an unsettling waving of her arms; as this movement is repeated with increased pace she suggests a bird trying to take flight, desperate to escape from some painful experience. She breathes heavily and her breath provides a soundscape of urgency. The whole piece takes place in absolute silence except for her sobbing, crying, breathing and screaming. She throws a spinning top to the ground and it spins for some time before it stops; she throws another with the same effect. In the end, Nyamza comes to stand behind a coffin-like box covered with a black tablecloth. She removes her suit jacket and, using a twofold image that evokes both a preacher at a pulpit and a politician at a podium, she leans over the table and glares at the audience until the lights go out. The repetitive nature of the work involves the 'sameness' that Nyamza refers to in the quotation above. This fixation with the 'after' in South Africa is no accident: it is a purposeful endeavour to make meaning in the period after-post-apartheid. In this 'now', as a period of recovery, we often hear the words 'struggle', 'pain', 'identity', 'wounds', 'scar', 'aftermath', 'after-after' and 'hangover', all of which suggest unresolved pain and a desperate need for re-invention. We are not through working on ourselves, we are not through figuring ourselves out; in fact there seems to be an increasing anxiety to work at this. In Nyamza's words, 'today's adult of 1976 is *re-living* and *re-inventing* those womb experiences of before and like her mother needs to continue to fight the good fight' (Nyamza 2013a, my emphases). Elin Diamond suggests that:

> While a performance embeds traces of other performances, it also produces experiences whose interpretation only partially depends on previous experience. This creates the terminology of 're' in discussions of performance, as in *re*embody, *re*inscribe, *re*configure, *re*signify. '*Re*' acknowledges the pre-existing discursive field, the repetition – and the desire to repeat – within the performative present, while 'embody', 'configure', 'inscribe', 'signify', assert the possibility of materializing something that exceeds our knowledge, that alters the shape of sites and imagines other as yet unsuspected modes of being. (1996: 2)

The material knowing of blackness is implanted in what is being performed: it is a physical knowing of a black woman's identity. That is why one struggles to separate the performer and the individual in Nyamza's case. It is not blackness alone that exceeds the performative but blackness in relation to 'other' in South Africa's socio-political and socio-historic positioning. *19-Born-76-Rebels* and *Isingqala* present the opportunity to *re*-work and *re*-imagine how 'after' is conceived and understood in the 'now'. Following Diamond, perhaps all performance relies on some kind of past, some kind of precursor. What the performative present exhibits, with the continuation of the 're', is the possibility of new territory. Even though the 're' calls back to itself, requires a 'going back to' something, it does so with the knowledge that returning to a previous experience can result in the birth of something new: this is the 'after'. Of course the past spills into the present, so that we also carry the pain of the past. Accessing that pain in performance gives us authority over the meaning of that pain in our present lives. South Africans think of 16 June 1976, not just as a historiography of the Soweto civil unrest (Baines 2007: 284) but also in relation to its after-images, rooted in place, feeling and in contemporary performances of the past, because the dreams of the protestors have not yet been realized. While Nyamza may be telling stories that recall the past, she does so to illuminate new contemporary problems. Nyamza draws attention to the way in which the past defines present identities, while bringing to light the danger of repeating that past.

NOTES

1   *19-Born-76 Rebels* has been performed numerous times. It debuted at Young Blood (Cape Town) in June 2013, was commissioned for the Festival d'Avignon (France) in July 2013 and later played at the Gordon Institute for Performing and the Creative Arts' Infecting the City Festival (Cape Town) in March 2014, and at the National Arts Festival (Grahamston) in June 2014. This paper references the live version attended by the author in Cape Town, June 2013.

2   *Isingqala* has also been performed many times. It opened at the National Arts Festival (Grahamstown) in July 2011, played at the Gordon Institute for Performing and Creative Arts' Exuberance Project (Cape Town) in May 2012, then at the Maison des Arts du Grutli (Switzerland) in September 2012, and finally at the Zurcher Theater Spektakel (Switzerland) in August 2013. This paper references the live version attended by the author in Cape Town, May 2012.

3   The Magnet Theatre Educational Trust is funded by a number of organizations, including the National Arts Council of South Africa, the National Lottery and the Arts and Culture Trust amongst others. Based in Cape Town, the Magnet Theatre's training programme caters for youths from various community theatre groups who struggle to be absorbed into training at university due to a variety of issues, including educational and financial disadvantage. See www.magnettheatre.co.za 9/1/2014

4   I often use the plural 'we' in my argumentation. This is because, as a black South African woman, I speak from a space of 'shared blackness' to the majority of South Africa's citizens in particular, and then I am addressing a global audience. As a writer, I choose to prioritize and foreground black experience.

5   Scarry herself goes on to challenge this concept, destabilizing the idea that there is only one way to think about beauty.

6   The article expressing these thoughts is available at: http://mg.co.za/article/2006-12-01-reconciliation-is-not-enough

7   *Higher Education Today.* An Interview with Dr Mamphela Ramphele. Video interview. 11 July 2013. Available: https://www.youtube.com/watch?v=ANyoMlclOew.

8   Backstage with Dr Mamphela Ramphele. Video Interview. 9 July 2013. Available: https://www.youtube.com/watch?v=az7r3L7vzFU.

9   Visit the TRC's website for reference to all official transcripts: http://www.justice.gov.za/trc/

REFERENCES

Baines, G. (2007) 'The Master Narrative of South Africa's Liberation Struggle: Remembering and Forgetting June 16, 1976', *International Journal of African Historical Studies* 40: 2, 283-302.

Boraine, A. (2000) *A Country Unmasked: Inside South Africa's Truth and Reconciliation Commission* (New York: Oxford University Press).

Brown, L. (ed.) (1993) *The New Shorter Oxford English Dictionary on Historical Principles* (Oxford: Oxford University Press).

Cole, C. (2010) *Performing South Africa's Truth Commission: Stages of transition* (Bloomington, IN: Indiana University Press).

Coombes, A. (2003) *History after Apartheid: Visual Culture and Public Memory in a Democratic South Africa* (Durham & London: Duke University Press).

Diamond, E. (ed.) (1996) *Performance and Cultural Politics* (London & New York: Routledge).

Forte, J. (1992) 'Focus on the Body: Pain, Praxis and Pleasure in Feminist Performance' in Reinhelt, J.G. & J.R. Roach (eds) *Critical Theory and Performance* (Ann Arbor: University of Michigan Press).

Grunebaum, H. (2011) *Memorializing the Past: Everyday life in South Africa after the Truth and*

Reconciliation Commission (New Brunswick & London: Transaction).

Henderson, C. (2002) *Scarring the Black Body: Race and representation in African American literature* (Columbia, Missouri: University of Missouri Press).

Hopkins, K. & C. Roderer (2004) 'Righting the Wrongs of Apartheid Justice for Victims and Unjust Profiteers', *Theoria: A Journal of Social and Political Theory* 105: 129-53.

Kamaldien, Y. (2013) *Dancer Mamela Nyamza in her own words.* Available at: http://yazkam.wordpress.com/2013/11/08/dancer-mamela-nyamza-in-her-own-words/

Launko, O. (2000) *Pain Remembers, Love Rekindles* (Ibadan: Opon Ifa).

May, J. (2014) '5 Minutes with Performance Artist Mamela Nyamza', *Times Live.* Available at: http://www.timeslive.co.za/thetimes/2014/03/12/5-minutes-with-performance-artist-mamela-nyamza

Masango, B. & G. Selander (2013) 'Born Rebels in Avignon' *Safari Culturel.* Available at: http://blogpartenaire-safariculturel.blogs.liberation.fr/blog/2013/07/born-rebels-in-avignon.html

Migraine-George, T. (2008) *African Women and Representation: From performance to politics* (Trenton, NJ: Africa World Press).

Morrison, T. (1997) *Beloved* (London: Vintage).

Nuttall, S. (2004) 'City Forms and Writing the "Now" in South Africa', *Journal of Southern African Studies* 30, 4: 731-48.

Nyamza, M. (2012) *Isingqala* [production description]: Gordon Institute for Creative and Performing Arts (GIPCA) Exuberance Project, 11-13 May, University of Cape Town.

—— (2013a) *19-Born-76-Rebels* [production description]: Young Blood Arts and Culture Development, 27 June, Cape Town.

—— (2013b) *19-Born-76-Rebels.* [Production Talkback]: Young Blood Arts and Culture Development. 27 June. Cape Town.

Pohlandt-McCormick, H. (2000) '"I saw a nightmare...": Violence and the construction of memory (Soweto, June 16, 1976)', *History and Theory* 39: 23-44.

Ramphele, M. (2006) 'Reconciliation is not enough', *Mail & Guardian.* Available at: http://mg.co.za/article/2006-12-01-reconciliation-is-not-enough

Samuel, G.M. (2011) 'Shampoo Dancing and Scars: (Dis)embodiment in afro-contemporary choreography in South Africa', *Proceedings of Congress on Research in Dance*, 40-47.

Scarry, E. (1985) *The Body in Pain: The making and unmaking of the world* (Oxford: Oxford University Press).

—— (1999) *On Beauty and Being Just* (Princeton, NJ: Princeton University Press).

Stent, M. (1994) 'The pillars of apartheid' in J. Harker (ed.) *The Legacy of Apartheid* (London: Guardian Newspapers) 53-64.

VIDEO INTERVIEWS

Backstage with Dr Mamphela Ramphele (2013) Published 9 July 2013. Available at: https://www.youtube.com/watch?v=az7r3L7vzFU

Higher Education Today (2013). Interview with Dr Mamphela Ramphele. Published 11 July 2013. Available at: https://www.youtube.com/watch?v=ANyoMlclOew

Youngblood. (2013) Video excerpt. Published 9 July 2013. Available at: https://www.youtube.com/watch?v=SWIlCU2cLw0

Jalila Baccar of Tunisia
A portrait of an artist

MARVIN CARLSON

Jalila Baccar is today generally recognized as one of the leading women playwrights and performers in Tunisia and the Arab world, and the work of her company Familia, co-directed by Baccar and her husband Fadhel Jaïbi, has attained a major international reputation.

Baccar was born in the old city of Tunis in 1952, just four years before that country gained its independence from France. She became increasingly involved in theatre during her school years. Theatre at that time was undergoing major growth in Tunisia, thanks to the support of the new President, Bourguiba, and the efforts of Ali Ben Ayad. Ayad was a Tunisian who had studied in Paris under Jean Vilar and was encouraged by Bourguiba to develop national interest in this art, which included encouraging drama in schools and establishing regional theatre centres throughout the country, following the French model of decentralization.

When Baccar graduated, she left Tunis for the first time in her life to join one of these new regional theatres, at Gafsa, the capital of the southwest of Tunisia, an historical oasis and mining centre. There she met Fadhel Jaïbi, then co-director of the company, whom she later married. They tried for several years to create a more modern and engaged theatre there, but were resisted by both the authorities and the more conservative members of their own company. Finally in 1976 they moved to Tunis, and established *Al-masrah al-jadid*: The New Theatre.

This was the first independent professional company in Tunisia and was deeply influenced by the French and German Independent Theatre movement of the twentieth century. Most of the plays presented were either by politically engaged European dramatists such as Brecht or new Tunisian works that reworked contemporary Tunisian history, filling gaps that the prevailing ideology or official discourse had created.

In 1993 Baccar and Jaïbi formed a new group, Familia, named after its first production, a Tunisian folk comedy about three sisters. Subsequent productions moved in a darker and more symbolic direction, as exemplified by *In Search of Aida* (1998) which is a symbolist quest play with a distinctly

Fig 1 Marvin Carlson at the National Theatre, Tunis, with Jalila Baccar, May 2014 (© Marvin Carlson)

political nature, insofar as it explores the question of Arab identity. The protagonist, played by Baccar, is a Tunisian actress who pursues the illusive figure of another actress, an exiled Palestinian, through theatres across Tunisia and Libya.

Baccar's work is significant in that it was able to engage with contemporary socio-political issues without being affected by censorship at this time when theatre was the only cultural form officially subject to censorship in Tunisia (until January 2001). All theatre productions, whether independent or state-sponsored, had to be authorized for public performances by the National Review Board, a commission of the Ministry of Culture, within which the Ministries of Interior and of Religious Affairs were also represented. Familia entered the new millennium having experienced no difficulties with this Board, and indeed was looked upon by the government as an excellent example of the success and sophistication of the experimental theatre of modern Tunisia. The major critical success of the play *Junun* (*Dementia*) in Tunis in 2001 allowed the country to showcase it internationally at that summer's Avignon Festival in France. It was the first Arab production staged in the 56-year history of this most famous European theatre festival. It portrays the encounters between Nun, a young man driven to schizophrenia by the abuse of an alcoholic Moslem father, and a sympathetic female psychiatrist, played by Baccar, who is locked in an ongoing struggle against a variety of patriarchal systems of oppression. These include Nun's family situation and the repressive assumptions of the leaders of her own profession. In a 2002 interview with a French journalist Baccar insisted that: 'We seek always to create a political theatre, even if that is not directly expressed in the text, and we reflect upon the most current concerns, those which the youth are addressing' (Da Silva 2002). Later in the same interview she noted: 'I did not choose the career of actress simply to perform, but to express myself as a citizen, and I often introduce myself as a "citizen-actress".' The term 'citizen-actress', which has a particularly revolutionary flavour in France, is often employed in articles concerning Baccar and her work, signalling her perceived role in Tunisian theatre and culture.

The enthusiastic response of the international press to this production gained the company an invitation to appear as the featured artists at the Berlin Festspiele in September 2001. At the centre of the celebration was the world premiere of a new play, *Araberlin,* commissioned from Baccar and written for German actors. If *Junun* reflected tensions in her native Tunisia, *Araberlin* appropriately focused on international tensions between Arabs and the West in the wake of 9/11 and the American-driven 'War on Terror'. In this play, Baccar returns to the character of the elusive Palestinian actress from *In Search of Aida* whose wanderings have now taken her to Berlin, where she has married a German man and is apparently happily assimilated. Suddenly, however, she is suspected of being the sister of a terrorist. A series of scenes depict her German Christian neighbours all turning against her, some eagerly, others with considerable guilt, until at last she is driven to leave husband, home and country.

In 2006 Baccar was commissioned by the Tunisian Municipal Theatre to create a work to celebrate the fiftieth anniversary of Tunisian independence. The result, *Khamsoun* (*Fifty*), was clearly not what the authorities had expected. Instead of a celebratory piece lauding the achievements and progress of the new state, Baccar's play presented contemporary Tunisia as a deeply divided state, torn by conflicts that independence had only made more prominent.

Although *Khamsoun* begins with a moving tribute to the beauty of Tunisia, this idyllic picture is suddenly shattered by a horrendous event: a young teacher blows herself up in the courtyard of her school. The police, fearing an outbreak of fundamentalist terrorism, arrest the teacher's friends and subject them to extended cruel and humiliating interrogations. One of these friends is Amal, the central figure of the play who, although the daughter of Communist political activists, returns from studying in Paris as a convert to Sufism. The religious tensions within Amal's family are developed alongside the increasingly desperate and futile attempts of the police to discover the motives behind the teacher's suicide. Religion, politics and the law become entwined in a lethal mix of fear, profiteering and struggles for power.

Although all of Baccar's previous works had dealt in one way or another with political matters, there had been few protests from the powerful National Review Board: that was not the case with this new work. After three months of deliberation a permit was refused and the playwright and director were provided with a list of 285 passages that would have to be cut before a permit would be considered in the future. Among the material to be removed were all dates, names of persons and places, Koranic quotes and all references to Tunisian history. This would have been like requiring the removal of all references to psychiatry from *Junun*, all references to Palestine from *Aida,* or all references to Germany from *Araberlin*. Baccar refused to make these changes and the play remained in limbo until Familia received an invitation to premiere it at one of the most prestigious theatres in Europe, the Odéon in Paris, where it was performed four times in June 2006 under a significantly changed French title, *Corps otages,* (*Bodies Held Hostage*). The play was a great success, although part of the enthusiasm it engendered was due to publicity which continually mentioned that the play had been banned in its own country. This allowed the French to demonstrate their superiority in artistic freedom over their former colony, all the more important because the victim whom France was protecting was a woman. Thus the colonialist dream of the white man rescuing the dark-skinned woman from her native male persecutors, most famously expressed in Jules Verne's *Around the World in Eighty Days,* could here be played out in contemporary terms.

In March 2007 the play was presented in Tokyo, which had welcomed *Junun* two years earlier. An article in *The Japan Times* boasted that Tokyo audiences would have a chance 'to savor it before those in its North African homeland, where the work is officially banned' (Tanaka 2007). Doubtless this growing international acclaim prompted the Tunisian government to reconsider its ban. In 2007 the play was approved, without changes, for performance at the International Festival of Carthage, to be staged by the Municipal Theatre of Tunis. This was a strategy the Tunisian government had followed with sensitive productions in the past, allowing them international exposure at Carthage without giving them access to major national or municipal theatres. Following a major success in Carthage, however, the play was issued a permit for performance in Tunis, although not for a solid run, as would be usual, but only for a certain number of nights each week. This authorization of the production in Tunisia without any cuts was a major victory against censorship, and for the dedicated artists responsible for that production. Indeed the history of the play, including its censorship, its success in France and elsewhere, and eventually its recognition by its home authorities, became a part of the play, and also contributed to Baccar's growing international reputation.

A new triumph for Baccar and Familia came in March 2009, when *Khamsoun* was one of two Arabic plays selected for the major festival of Arabic culture, *Arabesque,* held in Washington, DC. This first production of a play in Arabic in the United States was of major importance, but the very features that aroused protest in Tunisia ironically tended to reinforce post-colonial and post-9/11 negative stereotypes in the United States. While *Khamsoun* was less obviously anti-Arab and pro-colonial than Suleiman al-Bassam's desert sheik interpretation of *Richard III,* the other dramatic selection at this festival, it also depicted a society riven by conflict and corruption since the departure of its colonial civilizers. The fact that the work was for some time censored in its homeland, and that its author was a woman, also allowed the Kennedy Center, like the Paris Odéon, to play the role of the more tolerant and open Western power.

Baccar's next play, *Yahya Yaïch* (*Amnesia*), created in 2010, was conceived as a companion piece to *Khamsoun,* and dealt even more directly with political matters but, possibly because of the scandal around the earlier work, the new Minister of Culture, himself a former dramatist, was more tolerant (Lafitte 2011). Perhaps because *Yahya Yaïch* also contained fewer specific references to actual Tunisians, fewer substantial cuts were required, and the play was cleared for an April premiere. Still, Tunisian audiences were reportedly astonished that such a play could be presented. Baccar, recalling the genesis of the play, reported that 'Fadhel wanted to make it the trial of Ben Ali, and I wanted to try the whole population for their amnesia and apathy. In the end we made it a mixture of both. But we had great difficulty finding the right words for what we wanted to say; it took us a long time to shrug off the unconscious self-censorship, despite having fought against it from the very beginning' (Darge 2011).

The subtitle of the play became 'Amnesia', while the title character bore a name closely tied to the play's message, Yahya *Yaīch*. The original title, *Yaīch Yahya*, using the same terms in the opposite order, had prompted the only significant protest from the authorities. Yahya is a proper name in Tunisia, literally meaning 'survival'. *Yaīch* is much like the French *'vive'* or the English 'long live'. Thus before the revolution one often heard cries of '*Yaīch* Ben Ali', to be replaced during and after the revolution by '*Yaīch* Tunis'. The original title could thus be read both as an ironic 'Long Live Yayha' and as a potentially subversive 'Long/live survival'. Baccar and Jaïbi considered reversing the title, which would have preserved the double meanings, but chose to pacify the censors so that the surface meaning of the title was now a still ironic 'Yahya survives', while the punning 'survival survives' remained in the protagonist's name, signalling this extra meaning which was important in the revolutionary context.

The protagonist of *Yahya Yaīch* is a very contemporary character, a powerful caricature of a bureaucratic modern dictatorial figure (ambiguously described in the play as a 'high functionary') who becomes entrapped in a Kafkaesque nightmare of impotence. When the action begins, he is about to leave for an international conference when he is stopped at the airport, and without explanation returned to his home under house arrest. There he sees his fall from power reported on television explained only by vague references to 'abuses of power'. When he attempts to take refuge among the books and records in his library the room is apparently attacked by an arsonist, and in the fire, not only his books and records are lost, but also his memory, hence the subtitle of the play, *Amnesia*. Then, as a pitiable, suicidal figure, he is placed in a mental hospital where he is abused by doctors, attendants and other patients, and abandoned by his former friends and supporters. Finally he escapes from this imprisonment and flees the country to begin another life.

Amnesia was presented, not at Tunisia's National Theatre, but at the nearby home theatre of Familia, Le Mondial. Given the history of *Khamsoun* and the government's ongoing fear of civic unrest, the atmosphere at these performances remained tense. Jaïbi reports that Tunisian audiences watched 'frightened and wide-eyed'. Some 'turned around constantly to be sure that there were no police officers in the house, there to carry off everyone present, actors and audience alike' (Lafitte 2011). In fact, *The Guardian* later reported that every night 30 to 40 police officers attended a theatre seating only 450 people, but when it became clear that they were not going to interfere with the production itself, the audience received it with enthusiasm and joined in a vigorous debate afterwards (Darge 2011). A reporter from *Jeune Afrique* noted that the production was followed by 'thirty seconds of stunned silence and then a standing ovation' (Dahmani 2010).

The continued passive police presence was in significant measure due to stories widely circulated in the media and among the artistic community (most of which surely knew better) that the model for the unfortunate

Yahya Yaïch was in fact Tunisia's first president, Habib Bourguiba, deposed and discredited by the current ruler Ben Ali. Cleverly then, the play was promoted by its supporters as being in agreement with the current administration, its real target. This was evidenced by a major review of the opening night in the newspaper *Réalités*: 'The play offers a kind of judgement on the Bouguibian period, with its absolutism, its absence of democracy, its forbidding of freedom of expression and of the press and its different forms of abuse of power' (Zbiss 2010). The play ran on into early summer without government protest, perhaps because of increasingly frequent demonstrations against the oppressive social and economic system taking place elsewhere. For example, Karim el-Kefi, a member of the company, reports that: 'The theatre where we were performing was near to the Ministry of the Interior and the protestors often sought refuge in our auditorium. We were inundated with tear gas [...] The spectators were no longer able to distinguish theatre from reality!' (Lafitte 2011).

If the play was first seen, or at least promoted, as a political parable of the fall of Bourguiba, events soon provided an even more immediate parallel, making the play seem less reflective than prescient. Just seven months after the premiere of *Yahya Yaïch,* the self-immolation of a Tunisian street vendor in December 2010 touched off a series of protests that forced Ben Ali in turn to step down and soon after to flee the country. Among the first measures of the new government was the abolition of the censorship that had so long oppressed the theatre artists of Tunisia. News of these momentous events at home reached Baccar and Jaïbi while they were in Bordeaux, France, where a production of *Amnesia* was about to open. At that opening Baccar and the entire company raised their arms in a victory wave at the curtain call. All equivocation about the play's meaning now disappeared and it was almost universally now accepted as a depiction of Tunisia's current crisis, not an abstract allegory of a past regime. The *Guardian*'s review of that performance states unequivocally that the play 'details all the ills of Tunisia under the now defunct regime, with its nepotism and corruption, economic hardships and police surveillance' (Darge 2011). Within hours of Ben Ali's departure, the transitional government offered Baccar the post of minister of culture, a role at the heart of the power structure against which she and others had long struggled. Her refusal suggests how seriously she took her role as 'citizen-actress', feeling that her commitment would be better pursued within the theatre, the sphere she knew.

In the light of the rapidly evolving political events in Tunisia, Baccar was faced with the temptation to update *Yahya Yaïch* to reflect the radically changed political situation, but she did not do so, preferring to leave the script as it stood, an indictment of a failed leader on the very brink of a revolution brought about by his absolutist policies, and an important part of the archival records of that crucial moment. She and her husband also now began to consider this play as the central section of a trilogy on the Tunisian revolution, its causes and its aftermath. With the new order came new problems, among them outbursts of Islamic fundamentalism. In June 2011, protesting a Salafist attack on an art cinema in Tunis, Baccar made a statement reflecting her long-standing resistance to artistic repression in any form, which was widely quoted and became a slogan for Tunisian liberal intellectuals: 'We will not be silent, we will not be silent [. . .] We will not submit and we will not kneel' (quoted in Ballayeb 2012).

As the uprisings in Tunisia were echoed across the Arab world during the early months of 2011, and other seemingly entrenched autocrats like Egypt's Hosni Mubarak provided new parallels to Familia's dark fable, *Yahya Yaïch*'s reputation continued to grow in Europe as the outstanding dramatic expression of this new spirit in the Arab world. The Avignon Festival in July devoted a series of productions to 'The Arab Spring' among which *Yahya Yaïch* occupied a central if now somewhat anachronistic place. After Avignon the production was staged at other theatres and festivals in France, Germany and Switzerland, until the autumn. It was now recognized everywhere as both a major artistic achievement and an historical document recording the experiences of a county on the very brink of revolution.

Following the Avignon Festival, Baccar and the Familia company travelled to Germany, where they had been invited by the theatre in Bochum to create a new piece. Here for the first time Baccar adapted a classic text, Euripides' *Medea,* to reflect current cultural tensions. Her Medea was a Muslim woman from Anatolia, her Golden Fleece a precious illuminated Islamic manuscript. She flees with the Christian Jason to a dreary industrial town in Germany's Ruhr valley, run by the Mafioso-type Kreon. The play opened, with considerable success, early in October, shortly before the first general elections in Tunisia after the uprising, for which Baccar and her company returned to their homeland.

The first free elections in Tunisia were held in late October, and the Familia company returned for the first time since the uprisings to their native country to participate, expressing their joy that, in their sixties, they had lived long enough to vote for the first time. On the eve of their departure from Europe, Baccar and Jaïbi gave a joint interview in which they outlined the challenges that the current situation in Tunisia presented to them as citizen-artists. *Yahya Yaïch* was now successfully launched on its international career, with productions scheduled across Europe from Milan to Helsinki, and in the Arab world from Morocco to Syria, but it was already an historical document, and they felt the necessity to create a new work expressing the new post-revolutionary reality. 'We want to create a new play involving the young people who made the revolution, so they can have their say', said Baccar. The challenges were clear, because major new enemies to freedom and to the arts had appeared since the fall of the old order, and needed to be challenged.

While continuing work on this new project, Baccar and Jaïbi returned to Bochum in February 2013, where they created a staging of one of the most appropriate dramas in the canon to express the plight of living under a repressive political regime: Kafka's *The Trial*. This production began, not with the surprising arrest of Josef K, but with him already in the complete power of the malevolent forces that rule his world. He is wheeled onto the stage strapped to a hospital bed and immediately subjected to waterboarding, an all-to-clear reference to contemporary abuses of power. While *The Trial* was running in Bochum, one of the most prominent liberal politicians of Tunisia, Chokri Belaid, was assassinated on the steps of his home in Tunis by a religious fundamentalist. The night before, Belaid had predicted that 'All those who oppose Ennahda become the targets of violence',[1] and although the Ennahda-led government condemned the attack and brought the assassin to justice, the divisions in the country deepened. In the midst of wide-spread protests and a general strike, the Ennahda Prime Minister stepped down but tensions continued.

Under these circumstances, the production of the now completed *Tsunami* in Tunis was impossible. *Tsunami* in many ways recalls *Khamsoun*, although there are also distinct echoes, as Jaïbi himself has pointed out, of *Antigone* and her struggles against a cruel power structure (like Antigone, Amina loses a brother and defends his memory against a tyrannical uncle). Again, an older woman, Hayet (played by Baccar), and a younger, Amina, are at the centre of the play. The play is set in the dystopic imminent future of 2015, where Baccar and Jaïbi imagine that the religious fundamentalists, already a major force in the country and in the government, have further consolidated their power. The younger woman flees her orthodox home to escape from a forced marriage, and her path crosses that of a woman in her sixties, who, like the mother in *Khamsoun,* is a secular libertarian who has fought against repressive forces, both religious and political, all her life. In the end she survives, still resisting but eschewing violence, unlike the lover of her young friend, who returns to revolutionary violence when the latter is locked away by her family and religious zealots. The penultimate scene shows the establishment of a new government which closes all museums, theatres, universities and cultural centere, and all borders, suspending all civil and individual liberties.

Even though state censorship no longer officially existed, the work's unequivocal condemnation of the fundamentalists, and its specific reference to such open wounds as the crushing of the civic protests and the assassination of Belaid, guaranteed that it would be banned on the ground of posing a threat to public order. At that time even the name of the play's protagonist, Amina, was inflammatory. In March 2013 the 19-year-old Tunisian Amina Sboui (using the pseudonym Amina Tyler) had caused a huge outcry by posting topless pictures of herself on her Facebook page with the words 'my body belongs to me' written across her chest in Arabic. Extremists demanded her death and she was in fact eventually sentenced to two months in prison and threatened with committal to a mental hospital by her family. Although the Amina in the play does not use such extreme measures to protest, she clearly is a member of the same generation, with the same concerns, and even arouses the wrath of conservatives by her Facebook postings. To have staged it in Tunis at that moment would have involved author, director, company and theatre in a truly mortal risk, as the recent assassination clearly demonstrated.

Like *Khamsoun* before it, *Tsunami* was thus premiered in Paris, this time at the Palais de Chaillot, in May 2013. The Chaillot, like the Odéon, is a national theatre, today primarily devoted to dance and thus suited to most Familia productions, which often contain extensive dance sequences. Jaïbi was invited to serve as its international artist in residence for the 2013-14 season. Again, as with *Khamsoun,* success in Paris paved the way for this play to be performed at Tunisian international festivals, first at Dougga, then Hammanat, and then Carthage, during July 2013. The favourable reception in Carthage allowed it to be presented, without serious protest, in Tunis itself early in 2014. In all three festivals the play was performed in the ruins of classic theatres, reinforcing its references to Antigone. However, despite the protection afforded by the festival context, it is noteworthy that the name of the young activist in the play (whose Tunisian namesake Amina Tyler was then still in prison in Tunis) was changed to the more neutral Dorra. The name Amina did not disappear from the play altogether, though, but was shifted to Dorra's radical boyfriend, who returns to revolutionary violence after her persecution.

The play's Epilogue, however, gives a glimmer of hope. A young girl awakes from a recurrent dream in which she sees a huge black wave engulfing her native Tunisia. She seeks solace from her grandmother, who reassures her by saying that her dream was incomplete. A great desert bird heard her cries and flew her away from the catastrophe. When she asked him where they were going, he replied 'to the land of the survivors./Together they will restore verdant Tunisia/its colours/its love/and its security'. Thus the trilogy returns to the pun that resonates through the second play, *Yahya Yaïch*: 'may survival itself survive', and the determination that, despite all the setbacks, drives the indomitable characters played by Baccar in this trilogy. It also of course drives the theatrical project of Baccar and her bold artists, keeping them in the forefront of the continuing Tunisian revolution which today remains not only the first but still the most hopeful of all the manifestations of the Arab Spring.

NOTE

1   Ennahda, also known as the Renaissance Party, a moderate Islamist political party in Tunisia, is today the largest and best organized in the country. It won the largest number of Parliamentary seats (89 out of 217) of any political group in the first free election in 2011. In the eyes of most liberals, it allowed far too much freedom of activity to much more extreme Islamic groups.

REFERENCES

Ballayeb, Nourddine (2012) *Alakhbar English*. Available at: http://english.al-akhbar.com/node/8340 (accessed 22/5/2013).

Da Silva, Marina (2002) 'Interview with Jalila Baccar', *L'Humanité Fr.*, 16 September, available at: http://humanite.fr/node/30622 (accessed 22/5/2013).

Dahmahni, Frida (2010) 'Fadhel Jaïbi a bonne mémoire', *Jeune Afrique* (Tunis) 10 April.

Darge, Fabienne (2011) 'Amnesia: Review', *The Guardian*, 15 February.

Lafitte, Priscille (2011) '"Yahia Yaïch": Quand le théâtre rêve avant l'heure de la chute de Ben Ali', *France 24* 21 July, available at: http://www.france24.com/fr/2011079-festival-avignon-yahia-yaich-amnesia-fadhel-jaibi-reve-chute-ben-ali-tunisie-theatre-proces (accessed 28/8/2014).

Tanaka, Nobuko (2007) 'Drama despite the Establishment', *Japan Times*, 22 February.

Zbiss, Hanène (2010) 'La pièce *Yahia Yaich* de Fadhel Jaibi', *Réalités*, 20 April.

In Conversation
Interrogating & shifting societal perceptions of women in Botswana through theatre

LEBOGANG DISELE

Introduction

In Botswana today, the biggest challenge facing gender equality and women's empowerment is a patriarchal structure which mediates both our private and public spaces and promotes a hierarchy that vests power with the few, at the expense of the many: particularly of women. Patriarchal power is exercised and maintained through the silencing of divergent voices.

Theatre is a space where verbal language can be challenged by other embodied forms, which enable the exploration of the body and its relation to space. Theatre can provide a safe space, insofar as it is outside of everyday lived reality, and can suggest strategies for people to change their social situations. It can also create space for different voices to speak. Through the process of re-presenting our systems of power we can begin to address issues affecting women's rights and gender equality. Re-presenting means not only presenting in a new way, but also looking at ourselves and our problems differently, leading to empowered thoughts. It is only through empowered thinking that empowered actions can even begin to be imagined.

Un/Skin Me began as an attempt to locate 'myself' as a black woman in the theatre. Contemporary representations of black women in southern Africa generally have been and remain disempowering, with women often being portrayed as maids and victims, particularly of poverty. These representations are often reinforced by media representations of women which often fail either to give them any voice, or to voice their own life experiences. Instead, international and local media often present an homogeneous black female, who remains an exoticized, sexualized and/ or impoverished entity, often spoken for or about but never speaking for herself. Black womanhood has come to be associated with sex and struggle. This homogenous black female stereotype is the result of patriarchal cultures that continue to objectify and silence women. *Un/Skin Me* seeks to address these issues by interrogating the use of space, language and the body in the process of re-presentation. I refer to this process as 're-presenting' to signify a move away from existing representations of women which perpetuate negative stereotypes, instead presenting them in a new way.

Interrogating the use of space is about creating a 'thirdspace' (Soja 1996) in which multiple identities can exist and voice themselves alongside each other, rather than in opposition to each other. Edward Soja (1971) suggests that humans organize space in order to gain control of economic and political processes. In other words we act out power spatially, in both a physical and a figurative sense. He describes thirdspace as 'both a space that is indistinguishable from other spaces (physical and mental, or first and second) and a transcending composite of all spaces' (1996: 62). Soja goes on to list a number of different spaces including the ideological, imagined, political and real. *Un/Skin Me* sought to layer different spaces for each individual involved thereby politicizing the real, imagined and ideological spaces (at the very least) of the audience.[2] Further, thirdspace, in the imagined sense, is a mindset which, in Soja's terms, is a critical awareness that operates within a 'both/and logic' (*ibid*.: 5). It is a space that allows for openness, critical exchange and multiple perspectives. Thirdspace facilitates the process of delimiting possibilities, constantly seeking to break down boundaries and resisting getting caught in, or creating, new dualities. As such, the process of *Un/Skin Me* re-presented women by exploring the effects of layering different spaces for each individual performer. It also sought to break down the boundaries between audience/performer and stage/auditorium, viewing space/performance space, with a view to creating a thirdspace in order to resist and challenge the patriarchal order, which is often encoded in ways in which spaces are defined and controlled.

I use physical theatre in my theatre making as I believe that it empowers the collaborator-performer to use their skills, such as dance, photography and video making, rather than favouring the written and spoken word. Physical theatre is also a collaborative approach in which I can be a co-creator with those working with me in order to highlight and celebrate multiplicity by allowing everyone to bring their voice into the discussion, be it physically (dancing, moving, imitating/acting, miming etc.), vocally (singing, poetry, vocal scape, humming etc.), textually (writing, speaking), visually (drawing, photography, videography) or a combination of any of these elements. This approach allows me both to facilitate the performers developing their own thoughts and diverse views, and to engage with these ideas while also standing outside the work in order to shape the final conversation.

Physical theatre also creates a 'conversation', a two-way engagement between audience and performer, insofar as the audience has to make meaning from a performance that is not plot dominated and does not have a clearly spelt out meaning. This facilitates an interrogation or discussion of issues raised in and through the performance. It challenges the more common top-down approach to performance where one group (the performance creators) develops a work for a particular purpose and presents its ideas to another group (the audience). The significance of shifting away from this way of working is expressed by Sara Matchett: 'when one merges personal stories with master narratives, a conversation occurs. It is in the act of conversing that the potential for remapping old narratives to create new narratives emerges. This conversation affords one the opportunity of changing the old dominant prescriptive narrative that invariably places women in the role of victim or destroyer' (2007: 6).

Thus, a conversation creates a thirdspace in both the real and the imagined sense by encouraging performer and audience alike to interrogate their perceptions of women: how these are informed by patriarchal ideologies, and how they are performed in society. Conversations between the audience and performers allow the proposed topic to be interrogated, and thereby facilitate a re-presentation of the ideas.

Another issue addressed is who speaks for whom. As Jessica Lejowa states: 'very few of these women, of us women who are so often seen, described, studied, aided, donated to, are present in the making of academic discourse that pertains to us' (2010: 13). The silencing of women is evident both in academic discourses about women and in everyday life in patriarchal cultures, and it functions as a tool for exercising power over the female body. Thus gender discrimination has become inscribed in our everyday actions and everyday speech, reinforced by a barrage of media images that continue to objectify women. Henry Giroux (1992) advocates for the restructuring of language or the creation of new languages to allow subjugated identities to express and celebrate their differences. Creating a conversation empowers the collaborator-performers, as well as the audiences they engage with, to voice themselves. This breaking out of the constraints of patriarchal culture, to break the silence imposed on women and other subjugated identities, is important in contemporary Botswana. Creating a space for women to speak for themselves is a key tool for re-presentation as it highlights and celebrates multiplicity.

It would be wrong to assume that all black women consider themselves marginalized, either at all or in the same ways. Creating conversation is about exploring how we can use theatre to point out issues that affect society as a whole, become more aware of our own values and prejudices and where they come from, and understand how these prejudices are implicated in maintaining various structures of oppression and marginalization, so that we can begin to think about how to make empowering changes. Although my focus is on women, in Botswana the patriarchal culture mediates the life experiences of many people, based not just on their gender, but also on their age, marital and social status. The process of re-presentation therefore needs to involve people from all walks of life: men and women, young and old, rural and urban, in order to interrogate everyone's perceptions. This is particularly important because in Botswana the perception of defined gender roles is still an important factor in women's life experiences. Bringing in a male perspective also acknowledges that a shift in women's status in

Botswanan society necessitates, and is only possible through, a shift in men's status and attitudes.

My attempt to interrogate and shift representations of black women is essentially about exploring how we perceive the world, ourselves and others in the world, and about how we are perceived. Such an exploration requires that content be derived from the performers. Excavating individual stories allows for a collaborative process in which the facilitator-director can create space to engage participants and the audience in the process of interrogating and re-presenting images of women common in the societies being addressed. The process of creating conversation breaks down boundaries that maintain binary oppositions by moving away from an either/or language to allow for these shifts to take place: empowering women without disempowering their male counterparts.

Un/Skin Me

Themed rehearsals help get the conversation started by allowing the facilitator-director to raise specific questions at different points. For *Un/Skin Me* these questions focused on the co-creators, young men and women in their early to late twenties, mostly black, some with a tertiary education and some without, all with varying dance backgrounds, including ballet, hip hop and jazz. We began by exploring their views of black women, and how these views had been influenced by their own backgrounds (culture, education, economic standing, religion and political views) as well as by the representations of black women they have been exposed to in various media, both in Botswana and internationally.

Individual explorations of these ideas worked well to allow the collaborator-performers to interrogate their own perceptions, as well as locate themselves in the process. They also allowed them to experiment with different modes of expression, namely dance, song and poetry, as well as journal reflection. This is an important aspect of allowing the collaborator-performer to voice themselves as they begin to find what the theme means for them as individuals before trying to locate themselves as part of a group. This individual work was followed by group work in exchanging ideas and seeing how the responses fitted together. The conversation began in the rehearsal process, with a discussion at the end of each rehearsal, reflecting on the work that had been done, and sharing the thoughts and ideas that had come up in each improvisation.

Conversations do not involve the use of fictional characters, rather the collaborator-performers engage their audience in their 'heightened self,' a concept influenced by the ideas of Jerzy Grotowski who argued that the theatre 'cannot exist without the actor-spectator relationship of perceptual, direct, "live" communion' (1968: 19). Grotowski believed in what he termed the 'holy actor' who is stripped bare of superficial blocks and undertakes an act of self-penetration through a process of *via negativa*, a stripping away (of cultural myths, assumptions) to find the essence of what it is to be human. The holy actor uses their role as 'an instrument to study what is hidden behind our everyday mask – the innermost core of our personality – in order to sacrifice it, expose it' (*ibid.*: 37) thereby making a gift of himself in performance. The 'heightened self' is thus an identity in performance which allows the collaborator-performer enough objective distance from their story to be able to share it with other participants.

The individual work done with collaborator-performers during rehearsals allowed them to begin to find their 'heightened self' by locating their responses and exploring how to bring them into the space to be shared with other collaborators (other performers and the audience). Individual work also allowed collaborator-performers to take ownership of the work, strengthening the process of collaboration and creating a multi-authored work, which resulted in the layering of multiple texts. Structure is also an important component of the conversation. As part of the process of creating a thirdspace and new languages I try to avoid a linear narrative mode. I structured *Un/Skin Me* by naming each collaborator-performer's response according to the issue(s) they were dealing with, rather than creating a single narrative journey from the responses:

'Journey to (my)self' was an introspective response in which the co-creator sought a definition of herself, for herself, in which she was not aspiring to anyone's standards and could just be comfortable with herself.

'Kino Eye' was the name I gave to the work by a collaborator-performer who felt that he wanted to highlight the possibility and multiplicity of choice, using video. This involved recording each new conversation while we played footage of previous conversations on a laptop.

In 'Remembrance' the co-creator chose to retell the story of his late mother, who did not believe in traditional gender roles and raised her sons to do everything for themselves, moving away from the expectation and belief that a woman must take care of the house.

'A site/cite of confusion' engaged with how the collaborator-performer felt that young girls were not given the chance to grow into womanhood, but rather had it thrust upon them because of a biological change in their bodies, marked by their first menstruation. The collaborator-performer used photography to capture this idea, pointing out how gender is socially constructed and performed.

'In-flux', as the title suggests, explored a collaborator-performer trying to capture the sense of an identity or identities that seemed to be in flux. This resulted in a movement sequence involving full length mirrors, in which he seemed to be trying to find a more stable identity.

In 'A prayer of worth' the co-creator explored the effect of labelling on people, using a sheet to reflect the many ways in which she had been labelled.

'Find me (black) woman' was a title drawn from a poem written by a collaborator-performer which touched on the many labels she felt were imposed on black women, which then became fragments of words written in the space: on paper, on the walls, etc. It also became embodied through gesture: different poses/tableaux, dance phrases, running, sitting and so forth. The title of the conversation, *Un/Skin Me*, was born from these responses and attempted to capture the sense of not wanting to be defined by our biological make up.

For the final conversation we chose an art gallery installation format in which each collaborator-performer mapped their own trajectory in sharing their responses to the issues with the audience, as a further attempt to move away from a linear narrative. A gallery format allowed the audience to view each response in their own time, and to reflect on the issues alone before sharing them with others. By involving the audience as collaborator-performers in the conversation I gave them the opportunity to reflect on the other collaborator-performers' responses, then gave everybody time to explore their own views of black women, before coming together to discuss as a group, echoing the rehearsal process.

Un/Skin Me took place in the Moving Space at Maru-a-Pula High School in Gaborone, Botswana. This is a black box space which can be reconfigured to accommodate the needs of the performance. We used a minimal set to create a gallery space, similar to that of an art exhibition, with rostrums around the room on which the audience sometimes sat. This design allowed the audience to move freely around the room. It also allowed the performers and audience members to see each other. The configuration broke the conventions associated with traditional proscenium arch theatre (which facilitates a passive object/active subject binary) while facilitating active engagements and conversations between performance and audience.

In creating an installation performance we used the collaborator-performers' responses to make the space into a site of response. For example, in 'A site/cite of confusion' we hung photographs from the lighting rig, portraying the reactions of young women to the idea of the menstrual cycle. 'Kino Eye' resulted in two different uses of live video: we replayed videos of previous conversations on a laptop while at the same time the collaborator-performer recorded the current conversation. Juxtaposing a previous conversation with a current, ongoing conversation reflected a sense of needing to see ourselves and each other differently, rather than trying to limit definitions of ourselves. We also tied the black curtains in the space with white cloth to reflect the constraints created by the white sheet used for 'A Prayer of Worth'. As the sheet was a symbol of the labels we, as people, impose on each other, it portrayed how we become limited by these labels, and perhaps get stuck in them.

Reconfiguring the space as a site of response resulted in the conversation being multi-modal, resonating with the idea of 'Live Art' (Ugwu 1995: 6), which refers to work that is conceptual and driven by the expression of ideas, through the use of different mediums. Ugwu further argues that by 'subverting tradition and defying convention, live art invokes different ways of seeing, thinking and doing' (*ibid.*: 56). Thus the space accommodated and encouraged new explorations with each conversation and gave the audience an opportunity to share in the collaborator-performers' responses, even if they did not encounter them directly. A site of response is an open space in which the audience can feel involved enough in the process to share their own views. It created an opportunity for all those present to inhabit a thirdspace, by resisting easy categorizations of audience/performer or stage/auditorium, and by extension self/other, to try to break out of binary modes of perception.

Inhabiting a thirdspace meant that each conversation was a new exploration of the themes we interrogated. Aiming to enter into conversation with the audience meant the collaborator-performers could never know the outcome until we shared the space with the audience. Sometimes there were overlaps or intersections in co-creators' responses and sometimes the responses remained distinctly individual. What resulted, then, was a conversation that was constantly shifting because each new insight called for a further interrogation of the themes, a challenging of our own prejudices and a reconsideration of our own thought processes. Every new person had the potential to offer new insight by raising questions that had not previously been considered, highlighting the on-going nature of this conversation, thereby suggesting that the process of re-presentation is a continual one.

Conclusion

Our life experiences occur in and are mediated by space: domestic spaces, professional spaces, social spaces; and often we re-enact our lived spaces in the theatre, through performance. There is an opportunity for us, as theatre makers and theatre goers, to use the theatre space to re-imagine, re-invent, re-define and re-consider our lived spaces and through them our interactions with each other and the world around us. The process of *Un/Skin Me* sought to create a thirdspace in which multiple identities could engage in critical conversations about blackness, womanhood and black womanhood, but also about male identity and conceptions of female personhood, in order to re-present black women. Conversations in and through performance are necessary to challenge a patriarchal structure that operates by silencing those at the margins of socio-political power. Creating a thirdspace in which these conversations can take place encourages collaborators in the space to become critically aware of the roles they play in perpetuating gender discrimination. Thirdspace conversations thus re-present black women by empowering them to voice themselves and assume agency as subjects rather than being subjected to existing systems of power, particularly in Botswana.

NOTES

1   This article is derived from my Research Report, 'Working with Mophato: Interrogating and Shifting Representations of Black Women in Botswana', undertaken as part of a Master of Arts in Dramatic Arts by Coursework and Research Report at the University of the Witwatersrand. The full report is available on the Wits library website at http://www. wits.ac.za/library. The direct link to the online report is http://wiredspace.wits.ac.za/ handle/10539/12723.

2   The major part of the audience were students from Maru-a-Pula School, an independent secondary school, with other theatre goers, mostly academics.

REFERENCES

Althusser, L. (1984) *Essays on Ideology: Ideology and ideological state apparatuses, reply to John Lewis, Freud and Lacan, a letter on art* (London: Verso).

Aston, E. (1995) *An Introduction to Feminism and Theatre* (London: Routledge).

Bial, H. (2004) *The Performance Studies Reader* (New York & Abingdon: Routledge).

Birringer, J. (1991) *Theatre, Theory, Postmodernism* (Indiana: Indiana University Press).

Butler, J. (1990) *Gender Trouble: Feminism and the subversion of identity* (New York & London: Routledge).

Callery, D. (2007) *Through the Body: A practical guide to physical theatre* (London: NHB).

Elam, K. (1980) *The Semiotics of Theatre and Drama* (London: Methuen).

Giroux, H. (1992) *Border Crossing: Cultural workers and the politics of education* (New York: Routledge).

Grotowski, J. (1968) *Towards a Poor Theatre* (New York: Simon & Schuster).

Hill Collins, P. (2000) *Black Feminist Thought: Knowledge, consciousness, and the politics of empowerment* (New York: Routledge) 2nd edn.

Keefe, J. & Murray, S. (eds.) (2007) *Physical Theatres: A critical introduction* (London & New York: Routledge).

Lejowa, J. (2010) 'Shifting understandings of performance practice in an African context through auto-ethnography' unpublished MA research report, University of the Witwatersrand, Johannesburg.

Matchett, S. (2007) 'Shards of Memories, Fragments of Sorrows: Mothertongue transforming spaces occupied by women in South Africa through theatre', unpublished paper.

Oddey, A. (1994) *Devising Theatre: A practical and theoretical handbook* (Abingdon & New York: Routledge).

Soja, E. (1971) *The Political Organisation of Space* (Washington, DC: Association of American College Geographies).

—— (1996) *Thirdspace: Journeys to Los Angeles and other real-and-imagined places* (Cambridge: Blackwell).

Ugwu, C. (1995) 'Keep on Running: The politics of black british performance' in Ugwu C. (ed.) *Let's Get It On: The politics of black performance* (London: Institute of Contemporary Art).

CONVERSATIONS

Disele, L. T. Baatshwana, D. Kamyuka, A. Kola, W.C. Laba, C.T. Mangiroza, K. Saleshando & J. Williams, (2012) on *Unskin Me*.

VIDEOS

Mothertongue Women's Arts Collective (2004) *Uhambo: Pieces of a dream.*

Binti Leo
Women in the arts
in Tanzania

VICENSIA SHULE

Introduction

Looking at the story of independence of Tanzania, as elsewhere in Africa, performing arts, especially traditional dance groups led by women, were used extensively in the mid-twentieth century to deconstruct and openly challenge what Ruth Meena (2003: 148) describes as 'the colonial and patriarchal systems, which were based on ideologies of exclusion'. These dance groups, such as *lelemama*,[1] were significant during both the independence struggle and the post-independence deconstruction of stereotypes that perceive political power to be vested almost exclusively in men. Marjorie Mbilinyi (2010: 85) shows clearly that: 'It was TANU[2] women who forged alliances across ethnic and religious boundaries, who promoted Kiswahili as the medium of political discourse, who used local African cultural forms such as women's songs and dance groups to energise the nationalist struggle and make it their own'.

After independence, the 'energising political struggle' was transformed into women becoming the 'implementation tools' of the ruling party, TANU, later CCM.[3] This meant that performing arts, especially *ngoma* (traditional dances), featured prominently on national platforms when political leaders wanted to communicate social policies and political propaganda to the people. At community level such performances continued to entertain, educate, conscientize and communicate. Mbilinyi (*ibid.*: 84) further argues that: 'What is not understood is the degree to which this nationalist identity was constructed through the actions and thoughts of grassroot women politicians and activists, women who merged their struggles for individual dignity with that of a collective struggle for national autonomy and dignity as an African people'.

It is important to recognize these struggles by women on behalf of their sex, and for the nation, in order to situate and understand the role that Binti Leo (Today's Young Women) intends to play in contemporary Tanzania.

TANU women such as Bibi Titi Mohamed,[4] who participated in the political independence struggles through *lelemama* groups, had 'political' freedom and independence as their agenda (Geiger 2005: iv, 49). This was different from the women's movement in post-independence Tanzania prior to multi-party politics where most women had no space to advocate for their rights apart from supporting *Ujamaa*. (*Ujamaa* can be loosely translated as familyhood. It was the name given to the form of African socialism developed by Tanzania's founding president, Julius Nyerere, in the 1960s, which strongly influenced the country for some thirty years.) What is seldom openly spoken of is the lack of a women's agenda during the *Ujamaa* era. The assumption was that, because *Ujamaa* advocated equality, women would also benefit.

Ujamaa did not necessarily support a women's agenda: rather, women were the ones who supported *Ujamaa*. For example, most of the champions of *Ujamaa*, led by Julius Nyerere,[5] were men, and the first cabinet after independence was composed only of men. 'Political independence was the main objective for Bibi Titi and other women activists in the 1950s. Even though the patriotism and energy which they invested in TANU did not mature to give the power to control the state'[6] (Geiger 2005: 95). Reportedly, Bibi Titi realized that Nyerere did not honour the independence struggle's commitment to women. Ruth Meena wrote:

> When power was transferred to the nationalist government, the picture changed. Women's experience was no longer relevant to the post colonial struggles against neo-colonialism, imperialism and in management of the state apparatus. In a discussion with Bibi Titi, she ironically said 'I started smelling fish' when the first cabinet was founded. 'The highest post granted to us women was that of under secretary to the cabinet, which was equivalent to a junior ministerial position. When we asked Mwalimu, he said to us, 'where are those women with experience?' But quietly we wondered where [were] those men with experience to run the state?' (n.d.)

A good example of the long continuation of women's disempowerment was the banning of the National Women's Council (BAWATA) in 1996. BAWATA was officially registered on 16 May 1995, aimed at uniting women from all walks of life in Tanzania to achieve gender equality in a multi-party democracy. 'With the advent of political pluralism, it was felt that women might lose rights without an organ to voice their common concerns and problems' (Kapama 2009). The main argument given by the state for banning BAWATA was that the organization was not operating according to its objectives but instead had political ambitions. There were rumours that BAWATA was becoming a threat to the ruling party's (CCM) women's wing (UWT) in discussing and advocating for women's issues on the eve of the introduction of multiparty politics, and that it might even oust the CCM from power. In 2009 the High Court ruled against the ban and declared it null and void, and unconstitutional (Kapama 2009).

The exclusion of women's stories (her-stories) in favour of men's stories (his-stories) in the 'history' of Tanzania is one of the characteristics of patriarchal dominant thinking, as Mbilinyi emphasizes (2010: 85). The establishment of gender policy and a special ministry to deal with gender issues have been regarded by the Tanzanian state as key achievements and a vital step in the transformation of women's images and emancipation. Affirmative action has come to be seen as one of the solutions to the cultural and structural oppression of women. Special parliamentary seats have been allocated for women, education bursaries offered to girls in secondary schools, and scholarships and reduced entry mark requirements made available for girls and women to enable them to enter higher education, initiatives intended to challenge patriarchy in Tanzania.

In the post-socialist era women continued to utilize performing arts to inspire patriotism, advocate for development and to recognize and acknowledge both the individual achievements of various leaders and the collective achievements of the entire nation. A good example is the artistic association, Binti Leo.

The story of Binti Leo

Binti Leo was established on 6 January 2005 by 30 Tanzanian women involved in performing arts. Many of them came from art groups such as Parapanda Theatre Arts, Mionzi Dance Group and The Lighters, others were freelancers. Many founding members came from the University of Dar es Salaam and the Bagamoyo College of Arts (now TaSUBa). They range from those with only primary education to university graduates. The policy for recruiting new members has been to invite all women interested and working in the arts to join.

According to Joyce Hagu, a former Binti Leo Public Relations Officer and a Senior Cultural Officer at the Ministry of Information, Culture, Sports and Youth, the formation of Binti Leo had a long back-story: 'In fact, we didn't start collaborating in the arts. At the beginning we supported each other in kitchen parties and in different social ceremonies. Then, we thought why shouldn't we form a performing arts association since we are all performing artists?'

The need for skills training, and the autonomy to organize their work and gain reasonable financial recompense, were also key to the establishment of Binti Leo.

According to a 2006 Binti Leo brochure, the association's key objectives include the following:

- To recognize Tanzanian women in performing arts;
- To educate and empower them with knowledge and skills;
- To help them identify the important role that performing arts have to play in societal development and entertainment;
- To help them recognize the employment opportunities within performing arts;

- To open their eyes to the potential for economic empowerment through performing arts;
- To help them identify and understand their own importance in society;
- To conduct research and to recognize women in performing arts;
- To empower them with knowledge and skills to develop their art;
- To maintain records and an information database on Tanzanian women in performing arts and their capabilities in the particular arts they are involved in;
- To lobby for better policies which involve community empowerment through performing arts.

In addition, according to Hanifa Sabuni, a practising performing artist and designer who is also one of Binti Leo's founding members: 'We wanted to show [that] as women we can do anything without men'. Irene Sanga, another member, formerly of Parapanda Theatre Arts and currently a radio and television advertising director, adds: 'In many artists' groups, people think that something can be done only when there is collaboration between women and men. But contrary to this thinking we asked ourselves: if as women, we can play instruments, sing, dance etc., and we can form a group, why should we depend on men? Why should we have men in the group while as women we can do everything?'

Agnes Lukanga, a theatre practitioner and currently the chairperson of both Binti Leo and the Tanzania Performing Artist's Federation, speaks of the challenge women artists face when working with men: 'You know women need to show their artistic capability. They do participate in many art productions, but in the groups their creativity is most of the time overshadowed by men. Therefore there was a need to acknowledge the work that women artists have done in the society as well as their position in the society they live in.'

At the time of its establishment, Binti Leo's formal structure was similar to that of many artistic associations in Tanzania: it had a 'patron', chairperson and deputy, secretary and deputy, treasurer and a public relations officer. Membership then cost 5,000 shillings (a little over US$2) with an annual fee of 10,000. In 2010 the rates changed to 10,000 for membership with an annual fee of 20,000 shillings.

There were a number of women–centred initiatives which led to the founding of Binti Leo. A very successful precursor was *Tuseme* ('Let's Speak Out'), a project which aimed at empowering secondary schoolgirls' through theatre. *Tuseme* was initiated by Amandina Lihamba[7] and Penina Mlama[8] in 1996, and was coordinated by the Department of Fine and Performing Arts at the University of Dar es Salaam before being mainstreamed into the Ministry of Education and subsequently becoming a school programme in 2005 (Ndomondo 2005). The *Tuseme* model of empowerment 'came as a result of concerns amongst educationalists, parents and other social groups in Tanzania who saw that the academic performance of girls in secondary schools was less than satisfactory' (Forum for African Women Educationalists 2004: 5). Since many girls dropped out of school because of poverty, sexual harassment, unwanted pregnancy, early marriage or for other related reasons, it was clear that the situation needed intervention. The programme was mainly supported by the University of Dar es Salaam in collaboration with the Swedish International Development Agency (SIDA), the Ministry of Education and Vocational Training (MoEVT) and the Forum for African Women Educationalists (FAWE) (Ndomondo 2005).

Tuseme aimed at increasing the enrolment rate, and retaining and improving the performance, of girls in secondary schools. As a theatre process, *Tuseme* envisions a society in which girls (like boys) excel in academic study and are self-confident and able to fight for their basic rights, both in their communities and in the country as whole. Since 2007 *Tuseme* has been implemented in primary schools in twelve districts in Tanzania in a collaboration between the United Nations Children's Fund (UNICEF) and the Ministry of Education and Vocational Training (MoEVT). Some of the women who would become Binti Leo members worked in selected schools as facilitators of *Tuseme* helping students to use various art forms to express their problems to their fellow students, teachers and school communities.

The founding members of Binti Leo were also inspired by the female artists who participated in the production of *Twende na Wakati* (*Let's Go With The Times*), a radio soap opera broadcast which ran for fifteen years from the early 1990s with more than 1,500 broadcasts. Aimed at increasing awareness of family planning, the project was coordinated by the United Nations Population Fund (UNFPA) and the then Radio Tanzania Dar es Salaam (RTD), now TBC Taifa. Members of Binti Leo acted, directed and were involved in plotting the soap's story.

Binti Leo as an organization and through its constituent individuals has facilitated various artistic initiatives in Tanzania. A major project was *Tuelimishane* (*Let's Educate Each Other*), concerning HIV and violence prevention, coordinated by Muhimbili University College of Health Sciences, Department of Psychiatry, from 2002 to 2007. The project used mixed methods of drama, peer education and evaluation as a lay intervention approach for young men's HIV and gender violence risk behaviours, including unprotected sex and violence to female partners. The essence of the mixed methods approach was to enable youth to get involved and be informed of the different ways that violence posed a risk of HIV infection (Mbwambo, Maman & Nyoni 2007: 1-2).

The multifaceted nature of the intervention, and especially the use of community drama, were adopted to communicate sensitive issues. The intervention used skits which were performed in selected places in Dar es Salaam, especially the Kinondoni district where many young people spend their free time. After the performances there were discussions with young people and information was offered on where they could get more support when sex-related violence occurred. Members of Binti Leo were involved in both drama training and the facilitation of youth intervention programmes in Dar es Salaam (*ibid.*: 18).

Binti Leo in action

On Saturday 22 April 2006 at Nkrumah Hall, at the University of Dar es Salaam, in the presence of the Director of Culture, Professor Herman Mwansoko representing Emmanuel John Nchimbi MP, the then Deputy Minister of Information, Culture and Sports, Binti Leo launched its ambitious project: 'Recognizing Women in the Performing Arts in Tanzania'. This was an exciting and high profile event[9] that brought together prominent women in performing arts and arts stakeholders from within and outside Tanzania. As reported by regional art and culture journalist Ogova Ondego, 'the Association of Women in Performing Arts in Tanzania - better known by its Kiswahili name, Binti Leo – was launched with pomp and fanfare at the University of Dar es Salaam on April 22, 2006 though having come into being on January 6, 2006' (2006).

This marked the beginning of documenting the women in the performing arts in Tanzania, one of Binti Leo's objectives. The research was conducted in the five selected regions of Arusha, Dodoma, Kilimanjaro, Morogoro and Singida, aimed at investigating what women were involved in what performance activities. The research was supported by the Tanzania Cultural Trust Fund (*Our Reporter* 2006a). It was expected that the research findings would present the role of women in performing arts at a national level in Tanzania and perhaps reinvigorate appreciation of their contribution to national development, particularly in the fight against poverty. 'The project traces the role of women in the arts from the pre-independence era to the present' (Ondego 2006). The research report, which came out in 2007, brought fundamental changes to Binti Leo. It emphasized the need to unite all women in the arts, as opposed to the initial proposal to work only with women in the performing arts. All objectives were thereafter directed towards supporting all women in the arts in Tanzania.

The research findings showed that various respondents believed women in the arts should form one strong association. Quoting from the research report, one respondent from Singida region argued: 'We are doing arts. It doesn't matter if it is *ngoma* or craft, we all do arts. Actually if we don't have activities to perform we concentrate on hand crafts' (Sanga, Hagu & Shule 2007: 58). Another respondent in the report from Arusha argued: 'we'll be strong and have one voice if we have one association. If we divide ourselves, it becomes easy to be divided more' (*ibid*.: 8).

The research also awakened an enthusiasm in women to see arts as one of their sources of employment. 'Women are always perceived as mere housewives who have no role in productivity. But, through our performing group, we earn a little money. At least we are not sitting idle', argued a woman in Kilimanjaro region (*ibid*.: 28). In the report's recommendation the researchers proposed that 'there is no need to separate women in the performing arts from the rest of other women in the arts. In most places [where research was conducted] they do not feel they are different. They work together in the same groups' (*ibid.*: 62).

Apart from research and facilitation of various projects, Binti Leo produced and performed several plays, both in and outside Tanzania. A notable achievement was the performance of *Nkhomanile*, directed by Amandina Lihamba in 2006. The play was inspired by the story of Nduna Nkhomanile, the only woman chief during German colonial rule in the then Tanganyika in the 1880s. *Nkhomanile*'s programme states:

> From 1905 to 1907 there was a fierce fight by the people of Eastern and Southern Tanganyika against the Germans. This was the first war in Africa that involved many ethnic groups. Strengthened with their belief of support from the ancestors and the *Maji* (water) the people fought to drive the Germans out. One of the leaders who used the *Maji* to mobilise people was Nduna Nkhomanile. She was such a thorn to the Germans that when they caught her, they hanged her together with other leaders in 1906. This production is based on Nkhomanile's story which is little known. (Binti Leo 2006)

During the centenary of the Maji Maji war in 2005, historians at the University of Dar es Salaam published evidence that it was Nduna Nkhomanile who convinced other chiefs to accept *maji* (water) and use it as a weapon against the Germans. This challenged the accepted historical view that a male seer in Kilwa, Kinjeketile, propagated the use of *maji* (water) as a spiritual weapon against the German war machine.

Nkhomanile shows how the people of the then Tanganyika opposed colonial rule and, when they could stand it no longer, they rebelled and confronted the colonialists in a war of liberation. The play thus supports the argument propounded by Marja-Liisa Swantz that:

> Several books have been written recounting the life stories of the pioneering men in the history of Tanzania. In these books women have been conspicuous by their absence. Yet today's women leaders have been preceded by generations of women who prepared the way for them, and whose lives form an important part of the nation's development. (1985: 153)

Nkhomanile was performed in several places in Tanzania including the Bagamoyo Arts Festival (BAF) and Zanzibar International Film Festival (ZIFF). The play was also performed at the Women and Economic Recovery of Africa conference organized by the Parliament of the Republic of South Africa in Cape Town in 2006. *Nkhomanile* was a Binti Leo initiative which coincided with both the launch of a major piece of research about women in the arts and the Maji Maji centenary celebrations (*Our Reporter* 2006b, 2006c). As Ondego commented, 'if anyone ever doubted that women could defend their communities, these Nkhomanile warriors have cleared them with their shields' (2006).

The success of the *Nkhomanile* production was due to many factors, as Agnes Lukanga, the chairperson of Binti Leo, explains:

Every performance prepared by Binti Leo had its own position in the society. For *Nkhomanile*, the actors were all professionals and the director was Amandina Lihamba. We all know her capacity and experience in theatre. It was a big show with its own status. But I should say the outcomes were a collective effort and commitment from all who participated [and] there was money to do proper preparation. Time and resources used in that performance necessitated it to be of that higher standard.

Binti Leo has also contributed to the ongoing reforms of the creative industries in Tanzania. Such reforms include the establishment of four artists' federations, such as the Federation of Performing Artists, founded in 2010. Binti Leo members made an immense contribution to that process; one of the major achievements was that, in 'Binti Leo we managed to have the chairperson of the Tanzania Performing Arts Federation from our organization', as Hadija Chekanae, a performing artist and entrepreneur who is currently the association secretary, wrote.

The story of Binti Leo includes both individual and group successes. 'I've been very successful because many people have known me. I didn't know what TGNP[10] was [or] its transformative feminism ideology. Now I can moderate a debate, I can dare, I'm confident,' says Hanifa. 'I can support my family. I can send my children to school from just doing art works'. The increased membership is also a notable achievement. 'Currently there are about 60 members who respond when we call a meeting, even if not all attend: they send apologies. This is a major achievement' comments Hadija. However, it is a problem that few, perhaps fewer than ten members, pay their fees on a regular basis; and the association has not, as envisioned ten years ago, been able to establish chapters or branches in places other than Dar es Salaam.

The impact of neoliberalism

Starting with 30 members, at one time the organization grew to over 70 (Msungu 2006). However, there are currently fewer than ten active members. The major question is why? 'When we stay together, as women, we don't make progress', laments Susan Billa one of the founding members of Binti Leo. She had hoped that when Binti Leo was established it would bring positive change to the lives of women artists. But Binti Leo has not been able to engage many women, in recent years it has been unable to get funding and has failed to become self-supporting. This makes Binti Leo largely irrelevant to many women artists in Tanzania today.

Susan Billa further says: 'as far as I know, Binti Leo does not exist but five or six people can meet and organize themselves to perform certain assignments'. When probed, she added: 'the problem is, when there is an opportunity to perform, certain people only are selected to participate, these are the ones who are seen as Binti Leo'. It was noted that in many cases when Binti Leo gets an opportunity to perform, only a few members are picked and not all members are consulted on this choice. Responding, Binti Leo chairperson Lukanga denied such accusations, arguing that: 'for active members they are still enthusiastic and support the organization to move forward. For those who expected the organization to support them, their spirit is low, perhaps dead completely'.

In the late 2000s some members broke out and established 'Ten Sisters', a group of ten women artists. This group is little known and it is difficult to find any traces of it. The idea behind Ten Sisters, as identified by one respondent, was 'to revamp unity among women in the arts in Tanzania, and get more space which some felt they could not get when they were in Binti Leo'. One of Binti Leo's objectives is to unite women artists, but it is evident that for at least some members Binti Leo has been a source of disunity. Some members, particularly those with only primary education, feel they do not have the same 'share' as those with higher educational achievements. Here it is difficult to work out the probably complex influence of inferiority and superiority complexes among members, which seems to be at least one of the causes of disunity.

It should be understood that Binti Leo's establishment was a result of two major opposing global policies: socialism and neoliberalism. Women artists believed that there was a need to work collaboratively if they wanted to make progress and survive, but they struggle to survive in the current neoliberal era where the philosophy of 'the survival of the fittest' rules: the powerful and influential are seen as those who 'take it all'. 'If you go to mixed art groups, a woman artist is not valued; she is not seen as [...] contributing anything. At most she'll be costumed almost naked, paid two or one thousand [Tanzanian shillings]',[11] complains Hanifa.

A crucial factor affecting the level of Binti Leo's recent activity is the major policy shift in donor priorities: broadly away from funding culture and towards paying for security. The 9/11 terrorist attacks in the USA in 2001 heralded bad times for culture-based funding applications. 'As unrealistic expectations of western donors failed to materialize, however, support for African NGOs began to decline. This process was accelerated by the events of September 11th 2001, which prompted donors to redirect aid money toward African states in an effort to reduce the terrorist threat' (Igoe & Kelsall 2005: 2). This change in funding priorities was of particular significance for Binti Leo. Since its establishment the organization had been donor dependent: the Swedish International Development Agency (SIDA) was the main funder of many cultural organizations in Tanzania and across the region in the two decades prior to 9/11. These included the Tanzania Theatre Centre (TzTC), the Eastern Africa Theatre Institute (EATI) and the Southern Africa Theatre Initiative (SATI). The funding shift was not signalled to client organizations, so Binti Leo, like many other organizations, continued to send in proposals for funding, but in vain. As a result organizations such as TzTC and EATI collapsed, and Binti Leo began to be seen as increasingly irrelevant by Tanzanian women artists. Consequently interest and commitment waned. 'Sometimes if there is no activity, someone says why should I stay and pay [membership] fees? She decides to move on and do other activities', explained Hanifa. Lack of funding evolved as one of the major challenges for Binti Leo. 'We cannot run our programmes without funds. Donors have changed their funding policies. They want us to align and follow what they want. On our side, it becomes difficult [...] we cannot run training without giving participants allowances [for] their meals and transport', explains Hadija. Binti Leo runs various training programmes dealing with arts and the empowerment of women. Examples include classes in *batik* making, women's economic empowerment, costume making, acting, directing and scriptwriting, among others. These activities are ongoing even though they currently reach only small groups of around five to ten women, and only in the Dar es Salaam area.

Although the Binti Leo leadership is keen to raise funds, they lack a fund-raising strategy. Agnes Lukanga says they have a three-year action plan but I could not access this, and most activities appear to be conducted on an ad hoc basis. Responding to the issue of sustainability, Deo Temba, the Head of Communications of the Tanzania Gender Networking Programme (Mtandao), said: 'Most women's groups do not have enough resources so that they depend on TGNP resources [...] they need their own fund-raising mechanisms'. This implies that, although this major national women's organization is keen to support women in the arts, they do expect organizations like Binti Leo, after existing for a decade, to help support their own members.

Binti Leo is still marginal in Tanzania: it has failed to become a unifying national force for women artists. The major question is why? Leadership is one area of concern. Although it is claimed that they hold elections every three years, the leaders are mostly the same women who took office when the organization was established. If Binti Leo chooses to continue to operate as a membership organization, it needs more transparent leadership, with regular meetings and better involvement of members. Binti Leo could consider creating a less bureaucratic leadership structure, better fitted to take advantage of contemporary media, social media and funding opportunities.

A second issue is membership. Many Binti Leo members have 'abandoned' the organization for a variety of reasons, including poor leadership, lack of communication, and members' own busy schedules. Binti Leo needs to recruit more members from a wide range of performance backgrounds and to network much more effectively. It might be better to transform itself into a network linking up with women artists and their organizations, instead of the current approach which expects members to join as individuals. It also needs to re-establish itself effectively in Dar es Salaam before it seeks to become a nationwide organization.

Thirdly, Binti Leo might like to reconsider its objectives. In my view the objectives highlighted at the time of Binti Leo's establishment are still relevant: women artists still need a space to air their views and to raise a common voice to speak about their concerns. But Binti Leo needs to invite members and stakeholders to share ideas and agree how best to run the organization in a changed funding environment.

A final issue is financial sustainability. Since its establishment Binti Leo has not been able to identify any internal sources of funding apart from membership fees. It is unrealistic to expect anyone to pay fees to an organization they think is not useful or relevant. Binti Leo could consider operating as a business enterprise rather than an NGO. This approach might well be practical as most active members already have entrepreneurial skills and spend most of their time running their small arts-based businesses. Binti Leo needs to reconsider the possibly outdated idea that a woman-centered organization 'should' work as a charity.

Despite the challenges, some active Binti Leo members are optimistic (although many are not) and believe that they can survive and do better in the future. 'We are planning to produce short films which can be used to facilitate training in the villages. It is cheaper than sending the whole group to perform there', says Hadija.

Conclusion

Binti Leo has existed for a decade, and clearly shown its potential for bringing together women in the arts. The focus of its work is currently on training members in entrepreneurial and investment skills. The aim is to make most members self-sustaining. Members who are active meet up to three times a week to update each other about ongoing projects in various organizations in the creative sector. Most members have undertaken alternative activities to sustain themselves, such as catering, running small shops, and selling art works during conferences and festivals. Binti Leo is still alive, which is arguably an achievement in itself. It now needs to find new ways to achieve the admirable objective it set itself of serving all women artists in Tanzania.

NOTES

1 *Lelemama* is one of the women-only traditional dances. During the Tanganyika independence struggle women organized themselves in *lelemama* groups which became epicentres for women and entire communities organizing and communicating news about independence.

2 Tanganyika African National Union.

3 TANU joined the Afro Shiraz Party (ASP) in 1977 and Chama cha Mapinduzi (CCM, literally the Revolution Party) was born.

4 Bibi Titi Mohamed (1926-2000) was one of the first women to join the independence

movement in Tanzania (then Tanganyika). She was instrumental in uniting women through *lelemama* dance groups to fight for independence.

5 The first president of Tanganyika and later president of Tanzania (1962-1985).

6 English translation by the author from the original Kiswahili.

7 Amandina Lihamba is a professor of theatre, a playwright and a director. She has published widely in the area of arts, education, gender and culture.

8 Penina Mlama is a professor of theatre, a playwright and the author of *Culture and Development: Popular theatre approach to Africa* (1991).

9 I was among the organizers.

10 Tanzania Gender Networking Programme.

11 One US$ is equivalent to 1,850 Tanzanian shillings.

REFERENCES

Binti Leo (2006) *Nkhomanile Perfomers Tanzania* (Dar es Salaam, Tanzania).

Ernest, E. (2006) *Wasanii Wanawake Waunda Chama* (Dar es Salaam: Mwananchi).

Forum for African Women Educationalists (2004) *Tuseme 'Speak Out' Tanzania: Best practices in girls' education in Africa* (Nairobi: FAWE).

Geiger, S. (2005) *Wanawake wa TANU: Jinsia na Utamaduni katika Kujenga Uzalendo Tanganyika: 1955-1965* (Dar es Salaam: E&D).

Igoe, J. & T. Kelsall (eds.) (2005) *Between a Rock and Hard Place: African NGOs, donors and the state* (Durham: Carolina Academic Press).

Kapama, F. (2009) *Daily News*, Dar es Salaam, 3 April.

Mbilinyi, M. (2010) 'Reflecting with Nyerere on people-centred leadership' in Chachage, C. & A. Cassam (eds.) *Africa's Liberation: The legacy of Nyerere* (Kampala: Fountain), 77-92.

Mbwambo, J., S. Maman & F. Nyoni, F. (2007) *Final Report for the HIV and Violence Prevention Project - Tuelimishane* (Washington DC: Population Council).

Meena, R. (2003) 'A Conversation with Bibi Titi: A Political Veteran' in Mbilinyi, M., M. Rusimbi, C.S. Chachage & D. Kitunga (eds) *Activist Voices: Feminist Struggles for an Alternative World* (Dar es Salaam: E&D), 140-54.

Meena, R. (n.d.) *Gender and Political Empowerment: A Conversation with Tanzanian Political Veteran Bibi Titi*. Available at: web.uct.ac.za/org/gwsafrica/knowledge/bibi.html, accessed 29 June 2015.

Msungu, R. (2006) *Nchimbi kuzindua 'Binti Leo' Jumamosi* (Dar es Salaam: Nipashe).

Ndomondo, M. (2005) *Mainstreaming Tuseme in the Tanzanian Education System* (Dar es Salaam: University of Dar es Salaam & Ministry of Education and Vocational Training).

Ondego, O. (2006) 'Tanzania to honor women artists', *The African*, Dar es Salaam, 8 June.

Our Reporter (2006a) *Watafiti wa Binti Leo wapigwa msasa Dar* (Dar es Salaam: Majira).

—— (2006b) *Binti Leo kumuenzi Nduna Nkhomanile* (Dar es Salaam: Majira).

—— (2006c) *Binti Leo, BAWA kuonesha igizo la Nduna Nkhomanile* (Dar es Salaam: Majira).

Sanga, I., J. Hagu & V. Shule (2007) *Ripoti ya Utafiti wa Kuwatambua Wanawake Wasanii wa Sanaa za Maonesho Tanzania: Mikoa ya Arusha, Dodoma, Kilimanjaro, Morogoro na Singida*.

Swantz, M.-L. (1985) *Women in Development: A Creative Role Denied? The Case of Tanzania*. (London: C. Hurst).

Unnamed (2006) 'Binti Leo out to assist women artists', *Daily News*, Dar es Salaam, 13 June.

Odile Gakire Katese
Making art & reinventing culture
with women

Interview by ARIANE ZAYTZEFF

Rwandan artist Odile Gakire Katese was born and raised in the Democratic Republic of Congo (DRC) and 'returned' to Rwanda in 1996. There she studied at the National University of Rwanda and worked as an actress with Koulsy Lamko, a Chadian writer and director. She went to France and trained in theatre with Jacques Lecoq and at Le Samovar, then came back to Rwanda in 2003 where she worked as assistant artistic director at the University Centre of Arts and Drama (UCAD) until 2011, under the direction of Aimable Twahirwa, and then of Jean-Marie Kayishema. In 2012 she created her company, Rwanda Professional Dreamers, with whom she works in the performing arts, particularly in music, theatre and writing. Her current project, Mumataha,[1] involves the creation of two music albums and a theatre piece based on letters from a former project, The Book of Life, in which survivors and perpetrators wrote to people whom they lost or killed during the genocide.

Her artistic work was her point of entry into Rwandan culture, which she had to learn when she arrived from the DRC. Looking back at her trajectory and evolution over the past ten years, it becomes apparent how her position as an artist, who was also a returnee and a woman, has led her to approach Rwandan culture and arts with critical care and curiosity. This has resulted in a corpus of artistic work that speaks to the realities of contemporary Rwanda. Her body of work from 2003 until today[2] includes three plays: *Iryo Nabonye* (*What I Saw* (2004) as co-writer/co-director), *Des Espoirs* (*Hopes* (2005) as writer), and *Ngwino Ubeho* (*Come and Be Alive* (2009) as writer/director). It also includes the writing workshops of *The Book of Life* (2009, as facilitator); the albums and concerts of *Mumataha* (2012, 2014, as producer); and the drumming troupe Ingoma Nshya which she created in 2004 and has promoted ever since. As the assistant director of UCAD she organized a series of international workshops, called 'Arts Azimuts', in theatre, music and dance from 2003 to 2007. In 2008 she turned the annual workshops into the first international festival of performing arts in Rwanda. Through these workshops and the festival she gave young Rwandan artists

Fig. 1 *Ingoma Nshya performing at the Rwanda Drum festival, December 2011*
(Photo: © Severin Koller, 2011)

the chance to train with international professionals, and to open their minds to inspiration and creation.

In 2004 Gakire offered drumming workshops to women, at a time when this form was traditionally preserved for men. From these workshops, the troupe Ingoma Nshya (which translates as New Drums or New Kingdom) was born. Today the troupe numbers some 20 women who drum professionally. Gakire defines herself as a dreamer and a pioneer, and this project is a magnificent example of her commitment to attempt the impossible and to question what Paul Connerton calls the 'communal memory', i.e. the 'accepted narratives', the 'things that go without saying' (Connerton 1989: 18).

This article presents three interviews I conducted with Gakire in November and December 2012 in Kigali, in which she addresses her relationship with Rwandan culture, her position as an artist in post-genocide Rwanda, and the role of Ingoma Nshya in proposing a dynamic approach to culture.

Coming back and being Rwandan

Ariane Zaytzeff (**AZ**): Who are you, Odile Gakire Katese?

Odile Gakire Katese (**OGK**): I'm an actress by training, but also a dreamer. I like to say that. I've realized that I'm that more than anything else. I'm not afraid of dreaming big but I try to have practical dreams, every time. And because of circumstances, I became a cultural entrepreneur. So I had a short life on stage. At first it was a bit painful but afterwards I realized that my way of being useful was to be behind projects.

AZ: Growing up in the DRC, what was your first contact with Rwandan culture? How did the transmission happen? Was it through your family, or the Rwandan community? Or was there no transmission?

OGK: No, there was none. I mean, no conscious transmission, with someone making the decision to transmit.

When I arrived here I had to learn to speak less loudly, laugh less loudly: I discovered I was different. In the DRC, I knew I wasn't Congolese. Because everyone knew we were Rwandans. [...] When I arrived here in Rwanda, people still looked at me strangely. I thought to myself: 'Wait, I'm home, why are you looking at me like this?' People looked at me like this in Congo, but not here! I never knew why people looked at me that way, but later on I understood quite well that I was not from here.

For a long time I would say: 'You Rwandans'. Because I didn't feel Rwandan at all. For a long time I said loud and clear that I was from Zaire [now the Democratic Republic of Congo]. And really I feel like I'm from Zaire in my soul, in the way I approach life. So I had to make a conscious effort here. [...]

AZ: Do you think that today you've become a little bit more Rwandan?

OGK: I think so. I would say yes because I made this effort to appropriate my history. [...] [A]t some point it imposed itself, it went without saying. Even more so in relation to the genocide and its memory. [...] After the genocide, we also really needed people who were not here to bring what those who had been here were no longer able to give because they were so close, in so much pain. Everyone had an answer to bring. So I took this stance, to say: it is my history and I am Rwandan. I am able to question history with the distance I have, with everything it implies.

Making art to rebuild people and culture

OGK: Rwandans need a way of expressing what they will never be able to get out. Yet do we have such spaces to speak? I think we talked so much about unity and reconciliation in this country, we talked less about healing. We didn't do a true, systematic job of taking care of the psychological wounds, like we did with *gacaca*[3] for justice, and with unity and reconciliation. It is not about *finding* all the solutions but *looking for* them. We need to put the human being back at the centre of everything. We forget about it. We take so much care of the roads, buildings and palm trees. We take care of everything but the human being. It is true that we have access to schools, to medical care with universal healthcare; that is great. But a human being is not just that. There are wounds you can see, that can be healed. What happens to the wounds you can't see, the psychological wounds? That's a lot more tragic. That's why, when I thought of Rwanda Professional Dreamers, my whole argument was about damage to the mind: how the mind is wrecked. If we imagine that minds are in the same state as Rwanda was in 1994, destroyed, the same chaos is in people's minds. How do we then try to rebuild them? That's what putting them in the centre means. So that this man here, tomorrow, will be able to resist. A man is not just a body.

Emile Rwamasirabo, the former rector of the National University of Rwanda who believed in culture, used to say, and I like to quote him, that if we had had a dynamic and critical culture, we could have saved some people; some people could have resisted, said no, and not become murderers. He felt that in that sense culture could help people to learn to live together because peace is not created just by the force of an army or the police: the people who have to live together have to agree to live together. Culture remains a powerful way to convey this message. It was he who had the idea of creating the University Centre for Arts and Drama [UCAD].

The UCAD: bringing fresh breath into the arts

AZ: So Rwamasirabo created the Centre and asked Koulsy[4] to direct it?

OGK: It all happened at the same moment. He [Rwamasirabo] had the idea when the writers of *Writing for Duty of Memory*[5] came here. Koulsy's experience [with this project] in Rwanda had left a mark on him and he wanted to do more. They met, and Koulsy immediately did a workshop using forum theatre. Then he was selected to be the director of UCAD. He stayed from 1999 to 2002, then it was Aimable Twahirwa from 2003 to 2006, and I was assistant director. Jean-Marie Kayishema came in 2007 and stayed until 2011, I think. I was his artistic director.

AZ: How were the activities you proposed at UCAD received by the students, the audience?

OGK: From the beginning, not all the Centre's projects were necessarily understood. For example, the Ministry didn't like the 'Arts Azimuts' workshops because they didn't see the importance of bringing in foreigners to teach us how to dance, how to drum. We were always accused of perverting Rwandan culture, and that is something I did with great happiness. (*Laughter*) [...] But I know we were doing a lot more than that. For me it was about feeding a culture that was frozen and no longer had any content, or flavour. It was repetitive [...] and no one was exploring it differently. We hadn't brought in an outside eye that could come and look at our culture differently without necessarily changing it. [...] For me, as an artistic director who was creating the Centre through its projects, it was important to keep this aspect that is different. [...] Why would I confine myself to traditional dance, create another company, while there are many things to explore and offer to society? So we explore and do things that are different and have a lot of meaning; but of course, because it is the first time, there is always an immediate rejection.

I remember the first time we formed Ingoma Nshya, I went to collect the women's money, for their transport and food. I remember I had to undergo a very detailed interview so that cheques could be signed. [...] It was inconceivable for the authorities. First, it was not a useful project. 'Can't you take that money and make them a business?' That's more useful. Serious things. But beating the drums, what do you want it to do in their lives? It wasn't always obvious. Contemporary dance was said to damage the dancers' bodies, and then they were told they didn't know how to dance traditional dances properly any more. That's a concrete example to show how our work was received. You have a strong intuition and you know how things are done elsewhere because you have travelled to other festivals, and when you go home you want to do things there too. Yet sometimes, it's true, the audience is not ready. It's a way of learning, we learn with the audience. Sometimes they were not ready; sometimes the magic happened.

Ingoma Nshya: changing the place of women in culture

AZ: I wanted to ask you about Ingoma Nshya specifically. When did it start? When did you get the idea? Was it hard to set up?

OGK: No, it happened immediately. The only thing I told myself when I was at UCAD, when I was writing projects and wondering what to do, was that if I was going to do something, I would have to bring something new, not do something that already existed. What could be done to fill this cultural landscape that was rather empty at the time? Women were confined to traditional dance and quite absent from the arts. What was I going to inscribe them into? In the first call we published for women to come, we wanted to do everything: cinema, contemporary dance, sound and lighting, and drums. The only activity that really stuck, from the first minute, was drumming. The others frayed and disappeared. For drumming, we had trainers come during the Arts Azimuts workshops which we were able to run for six months. We had the drums, too. We had the space. We had women who, from the first moment they touched the drums, loved it. They couldn't wait to come back the next day. They didn't want to leave rehearsal and go home. We had to chase them out to close the room and they couldn't wait until the next day. That is how it started, very easily.

AZ: Were there male drumming troupes at the time?

OGK: Yes. Well, in every traditional dance company there are always drummers. Even the drummers who come to the Rwanda Drum Festival, they come from dance. There aren't really companies that exclusively play drums. They do dance because I think it is easier to earn money from it, performing at weddings. […] Whereas if you only drum, how can you survive? They know how to drum but they don't do it professionally. They don't invest as much as Ingoma Nshya does.

Challenging tradition

AZ: Why couldn't women play, traditionally?

OGK: Precisely. When I asked around, I couldn't get a serious answer. People were telling me it was because it was too heavy, which I do not take seriously. Originally, it wasn't even all men who could play drums. It was only men who were worthy of the drums, at the royal court, who were carefully selected. And drumming was only performed for the king. So women were excluded from that space. With time, it became one of these interdictions that we don't question because it's been forbidden forever, why should we question it today? The king is no longer here, women are doing new things, but still we don't question it.

AZ: Did the idea of creating a women's troupe come naturally after the workshops?

OGK: Yes. It was in 2004. Once the six months of training were over the women didn't work as regularly and they did not keep up the same standards, the same rigour as before. We couldn't pay for transport or anything so they came on their own terms, when they wanted to and could. Yet, despite all these difficulties, it didn't fray. Women didn't come every day but they were here, they kept coming. Until we could create a programme for them and had the money to structure all that. We absolutely had to involve women, who were the great absence in artistic activities. And one of the first things we did was to have a woman drummer [Ndeye Seck] come from Ecole des Sables in Senegal to train them. And to show them that there was a woman in Senegal who was doing just that. It had a positive impact, yet it was too much for the women. The level was too high, too hard to remember. We were not ready. But we met our objectives because she hadn't come just to train the women but also to comfort them, if they felt discouraged. Or to show those who thought it was easy that no, it was an art, a craft. She brought a lot of answers that we needed, but in terms of rhythms we didn't keep anything. That was in 2007. In January 2008, Doudou N'Diaye Rose came for the Arts Azimuts festival and he gave workshops to the women. It went great. Even today we can still tell: this rhythm is Senegalese. Even in the gestures, the way of beating the drums: a transmission of technique happened. Maybe we were ready; maybe it was easier, I don't know. That is when things became serious and we decided to make something of it.

AZ: Is that when you chose a name or did you have a name already?

OGK: At first we were called 'Women's Initiative'. Ingoma Nshya [New Drum/New Kingdom] came later; I remember thinking that we needed a Rwandan name, but I don't remember when it was exactly.

Changing the drums with women

AZ: Why Ingoma Nshya?

OGK: Ingoma Nshya because that's what we were doing, proposing a new drum, played by women. In the political context also: the background is that we are in a new regime in which women are authorized to touch the drums. Can they be authorized to do things, really, after the genocide? Women end up as heads of family; they *have* to do a lot of things. Yet, among these things, they do not have to play drums, but they can. Why not? I think that's why it did not create a big stir to see women drumming. After a tragedy like the genocide that broke so many taboos, was it [drumming] really the taboo about which we were shocked? Women were taking on responsibilities they had never had before because of the conditions they were living in, so if they wanted to drum, it was not that important. This also acknowledges a political will that lets women do things. People want women to do more, to take more initiatives. The name Ingoma Nshya also came from the fact that from the first day we touched the drums (I drummed too in the beginning) it was clear to us that drumming was about to change, thanks to women, thanks to us. The idea of being the first Rwandan women drummers was also a beautiful motivation.

So it was not the same drum. Even politically, it was no longer the same drum; things were changing. Women were proposing a new drum. There was an idea that drumming could be reborn through women, regain strength, be rejuvenated, and get some air. I was conscious that women were really going to change things. When we created the drum festival, I was very happy that it was women who were inviting men to drum. It was a new space that women could invade and they could do what they wanted with it, to find more freedom, more fun.

AZ: You say that women changed the drums. How exactly? What did you notice that people are doing differently, what is the influence of women? For example, in June [2012] when 150 drummers performed in town, I noticed that some troupes had women too, alongside men. Beyond the gender aspect, do you find that there are other changes?

OGK: Yes. First, I found that, before us, men played drums with a certain casualness. I saw that during the first Rwanda Drum Festival. They were very confident. Because we were the hostesses, we let everyone perform before us. After their performances, we performed and they saw that what we were doing was serious. What we presented at the end of the first day showed this, and it was clear on the second day that they were trying to be more organized. They wanted to be the best: it's normal, we want that too. Ingoma Nshya prepared themselves so seriously precisely because it wasn't something we were entitled to do: we had to take it. So we were afraid of the men who had been playing drums for centuries; we were not sure that we were ready. Yet because the men do not practise drumming regularly, you can feel it in the quality. In addition, Ingoma Nshya opened up to the world: they had training sessions with a Senegalese drummer, a Brazilian drummer, etc. When they perform, it is something quite refreshing. Whereas with the men, it is the same things that we already know, the same line of drums. Women had shaken that up already. As a result, the second and third festivals were not the same and the men had prepared seriously before coming. They approached drums with rigour.

AZ: What about the movements? Was it usual to move and dance while drumming?

OGK: Traditionally, and until today, men stand in a line and just drum. But the gestures, the movement, that wasn't Ingoma Nshya, that was UCAD. And that's what I loved about it. The first dance workshop, for example, was called: 'make me dance differently'. And I think everything we have done since then at UCAD was 'make me do this differently'. Make me drum, make me do theatre: make me dream, in a word. The objective was to nourish the imagination of the artists. Ingoma Nshya was born in that centre and its members live around it, so they see a lot of different things. When we started drumming – and the drums are quite heavy – we looked for ways to pick up the drums and move them, to break that line. We thought a lot about how to make the drums move. Then we thought: if we can't move them much, we can move ourselves around them, to make it more interesting. That's why I was very touched by the work that Carlos from Brazil did. The first time that I saw the choreography, I cried. Even in my imagination I was wondering what he was going to do because I'm not a choreographer so I have a hard time dreaming about these things. When they first showed me I was shocked, in a positive way, so much so that I cried.

Creating traditional culture in the present

AZ: What were the reactions when you created Ingoma Nshya? You seem to be saying that there was no real shock, but does that mean there were only positive reactions? Or were there people who thought you were going too far?

OGK: At the beginning a lot of men came to see the women drum and they laughed out loud because they didn't know what [the women] were doing. At the very beginning we were terrible at drumming. That was a lot of fun for men, who thought we couldn't do it. There was also a problem with the noise. That's why I say that before Ingoma Nshya people didn't play drums so regularly. It wasn't a daily job: people only rehearsed for special events. So we had a lot of complaints about the noise; we were making a lot of noise. I thought it was good that women were speaking up in that sense too, in such a loud way. But we are in a country that has a strong gender policy and favours women's initiatives. Which authority could have come and told us that we couldn't drum? It was impossible. On the contrary, once the women started mastering the drums and performing, everyone wanted to be seen with them because it became an image of what was being done in the country. Then, with the Ministry of Sports and Culture [...] they didn't do anything against us, but we are not a troupe that they invite to their events. We've never had an invitation from them except when they want us to perform with men, when they want 200 drummers. Because the women are accused of not performing Rwandan drumming: they mix rhythms. It is true that symbolically, in the past, when a territory was invaded or a war was won, they played the drums of the conqueror. So if we play rhythms from Burundi, it means they are the masters here. That's why I understand, politically, why they wouldn't want us to play rhythms from Burundi at a political event. The word 'Ingoma' involves not just the drum but also the political power. The Ministry wants to preserve tradition in a static way, to keep it intact. So first, in Ingoma Nshya, they are women, they have broken a taboo, that's a bad start. Then what they do is not exactly what used to be done. Yet do we confine ourselves to that? The practice within which we are confined will dry out. In the performing arts, it is not possible to exist if we just reproduce. We are aware of where we come from, but in order to continue and still be here five years later, we can't stay still. An artist must create: that's her job. To me, Ingoma Nshya's drum is Rwandan, of course. Ingoma Nshya brought everyone back to the essential: a drummer's work is making and playing rhythms. How can you reproach people working seriously to create a new rhythm, and refuse it because that's not the way it has been done before? It was fossilized. We seem to forget that as drummers, artists, but also as citizens, we have received a heritage but that heritage is not meant to be preciously kept intact. We need to bring our contribution to this heritage to enrich it and transmit it to the next generations. Otherwise people end up with things that have no content: skeletons. We don't remember why we do it so it cannot enrich people. The culture becomes poorer with time because we do not bring our contribution, which does not have to be extraordinary but human. It is not about being revolutionary, it is about small contributions, odd or inappropriate stories that come to shake things up and change our route.

AZ: Who had the idea of the Rwanda Drum Festival [RDF]? How did it happen?

OGK: I did. For the first festival, we had spent almost a year training a new group of women but we didn't know how to end the training. Where were we going to perform? At that time, in 2008, the women didn't have the same reputation as today. Even today, they are not invited much to drum in the country. For me it was essential that they could exist at home. So we decided that if people didn't invite us – and to tell the truth there were not many festivals or occasions at which to perform – let's create our own festival. We need a drum festival, too. We invited ourselves, and we then immediately had 127 participants. For me it is important to start, no matter how you start. Then you learn to structure things. And it was impressive. For the second festival we invited 100 participants, from every province; for the third festival we invited only 40 because we couldn't afford 100; the third festival, I don't know, 60 maybe. When I started Ingoma Nshya I knew they were the first women drummers in Rwanda, but when I created RDF I hadn't realized that it was the first national festival. And to this day I am shocked that there is no national festival in Rwanda. Even the Ministry of Sports and Culture, at least, could have a small national festival. I understand clearly why culture is quite static here.

A project with multiple and unforeseen meanings: From joy to reconciliation

AZ: Very often, Ingoma Nshya is perceived as a reconciliation project because Hutu and Tutsi women drum together. Yet that was not the original goal at all. Does it bother you? Do you embrace it?

OGK: It doesn't bother me at all. I say I focus on projects about the genocide every five years, but I know that everything remains part of the post-conflict context. Everything takes root in that. Some projects surprise you. Reconciliation was never an objective; it was a project for women. Then the women who came to do this came with their backgrounds: one's father was in prison, another was an orphan and didn't know where to sleep, and another one had been beaten by her husband [...] It became a way out; that was very important to them. We never consciously formulated it but they felt good together. What mattered was not who they were but what they were doing. They felt supported. It took on a meaning we hadn't foreseen.

In the beginning it was about women. I always complain about the fact that life is too serious and leisure is not a priority; we don't make time for that. Even in Kinyarwanda there are no words for this: it's about accepting, *kwihangana* [being patient, enduring] etc. Now, women's lives in particular are worse than that. They are confined at home, especially outside of Kigali. They have no prospects and are not given the tools to dream or to want something else. For me it is important to bring some air, some joy. The notion of joy, of pleasure, we gave it up very quickly and very naturally. And nobody even thinks about it. So why do you want women to play drums? Well, because it brings them pleasure, first. Because it is exhilarating, it's ... oh my god, it's fun to play drums! First of all, I would like to answer just this. But then, I can't just leave the answer at that. I have a lot of reasons and motivations at different levels, and that's good too. Yet this space remains a parenthesis into which we escape to rest, and then we return to the same old life that hasn't changed. Women in particular need that. It was a space in which there were no men to tell them how to do things, how to behave, or what they couldn't do. They will make their own rules.

It remains a project that became very meaningful. It revealed itself with time; it turned out to make a lot of sense. Every time,

I thought: wow, what a beautiful idea to have thought of this and created that troupe, because it had to be done. It had to be done and we're happy we did it. Yet it has meaning at several levels, be it to open a new page in the history of the country, which I am incredibly proud of. Every time I would tell the women: it will be your names; you will be the first women drummers in Rwanda. It also has meaning at the level of helping women broaden their future prospects. It also has meaning in their own lives, learning how to hold their heads up and change their way of walking, of comprehending people, life [...] Then, if it illustrates the realities of Rwanda where everyone lives together in spite of everything, that has meaning too. It's one of the rare projects which makes me feel very useful.

ACKNOWLEDGEMENT

The author gratefully acknowledges the Fondation pour la Mémoire de la Shoah's support of the research which led to this article.

NOTES

1   The Kinyarwanda word *Mumataha* is not readily translatable. It refers to the moment, at dusk, when the cowherds bring the cattle back and everyone gathers around the fire to share stories.
2   Her work as an actress was particularly important from 1999 to 2001, but this article focuses on her work as a director and producer.
3   The local tribunals, which tried perpetrators of genocide from 2002 to 2012.
4   Koulsy Lamko is a Chadian writer and playwright. He left Chad because of the civil war and lived in Burkina Faso for 10 years, where he worked in community theatre, before coming to Rwanda. He was the first director of UCAD.
5   *Ecrire par Devoir de Mémoire* was a writing project organized by Fest'Africa which brought ten African writers to Rwanda in 1998 and 2000 and invited them to write about the 1994 genocide against the Tutsi. Koulsy Lamko first came to Rwanda with this project.

REFERENCES

Connerton, Paul (1989) *How Societies Remember* (New York: Cambridge University Press).
Gakire, Odile Katese (4 December 2012), interview with author. Kigali, interview 1, transcript. Translated from French by Ariane Zaytzeff.
——— (8 December 2012), interview with author. Kigali, interview 2, transcript. Translated from French by Ariane Zaytzeff.
——— (9 December 2012), interview with author. Kigali, interview 3, transcript. Translated from French by Ariane Zaytzeff.

Contemporary
Ethiopian Actresses

JANE PLASTOW & MAHLET SOLOMON[1]

Introduction

Ethiopia is an interesting place to look at the changing lives of actresses[2] in Africa, both because it has the longest and strongest tradition of state supported theatre houses anywhere on the continent, and because it has moved from a time when, prior to 1951, all parts were played by men, to a present when leading actresses can be nationally recognized 'stars'.

The first modern play, written like nearly all Ethiopian theatre in Amharic, dates back to 1921,[3] and was performed by a cast of schoolboys. Play writing subsequently became a fashion among the aristocrats of the court of the last Ethiopian Emperor, Haile Selassie, in the 1930s, and the first professional theatre, the Hager Fikir, was established in the 1940s, followed shortly afterwards by the City Hall Theatre, and in 1955 by the 1,400-seat Haile Selassie 1 Theatre (now the National Theatre with a staff of over 200).[4] Ever since that time theatre-going has been a part of life in the capital Addis Ababa, which currently has five major theatres (though only two were operating fully at the time of writing) with productions also mounted by private companies in a number of halls, and tours regularly undertaken to major cities around the country. At times theatre has played a major political role in agitating for change, and since 1974 the companies in the state theatres have been government employees on recognized salary scales and with full pension rights.[5] A number of attempts to create theatre training schemes have been made since the 1960s, but nowadays most actors, playwrights and directors are graduates of the Theatre Arts Department of Addis Ababa University, which began offering degree courses in 1978.[6]

Ethiopian plays are put on in repertory. A play is normally performed once a week and a run may last for up to three years. Theatre houses put on a number of plays simultaneously, with the largest number being performed at the National Theatre where shows take place every day except Monday, with two performances on Saturdays and Sundays. Ticket

97

prices are regulated, and recently there has been a battle between theatre professionals and the government which wanted to hold prices down to 15 birr (approximately US$ 0.60). In 2015 prices have risen to 40 birr (US$ 1.80). The bulk of audiences are youngish middle or lower middle class city dwellers, with a preponderance of young men.

Traditionally Ethiopia honoured playwrights but despised performers, who in the early days were either schoolboys or *azmaris*, drawn from a caste grouping of musicians and singers. In a strongly patriarchal culture it has been extremely hard for women to gain respect as performers. The first (and still one of very few) women playwrights was Sennedu Gebru, a pioneer of female education who wrote some twenty patriotic and socially oriented plays to be performed by girls at the Empress Menen Girls' High School where she was headmistress between 1947 and 1955.[7] This was seen as acceptable because the performances were only for pupils and invited, high ranking audiences. In the professional theatres producers struggled for years to find a woman bold enough to defy mores that confined respectable women to domestic life. Men were forced to play female roles, which they found deeply humiliating,[8] until in 1951 Selamawit Gebresellasie was persuaded to appear as the legendary Queen of Sheba. Still, women on stage were regarded as immoral and were generally lower class until female students began to graduate with Theatre Studies degrees in the 1980s. Few of the initial trickle of students chose theatre as their degree course of preference, and many felt compelled to lie to their parents about what they were doing, at least until they graduated, although the situation is now very different and most female students enrol on theatre courses with parental approval.[9]

When Jane Plastow first undertook research among female performers in Ethiopia in the 1980s their status was only just beginning to rise, and no respectable man would have been willing to marry an actress, although many, including numerous directors, sought to sleep with them, sometimes as the price of giving them a role in a play. The few actresses who were married at that time had husbands in the same profession. Some of the older directors refused to employ women graduate actresses because they were not amenable to sexual overtures. However, from the 1980s onwards female graduates such as Jemanesh Solomon and Elizabeth Melaku were keen to assert their professional status, and demanded respect and a creative voice in the productions in which they participated. The first all-female directed and acted production took place only in 2006, when Azeb Worku put on a comedy by Robert Thomas, translated from French: *Semintu Setoch (Huit Femmes)* which ran successfully at the National Theatre for eighteen months before going on tour.[10] Nowadays, and especially since the birth of a popular national film industry in the twenty-first century, leading actresses are national celebrities. The perceived glamour of the profession has attracted many new entrants, although most actresses continue to occupy a financially and socially precarious position.

The actresses

Six women kindly agreed to be interviewed by Mahlet Solomon for this article in September 2014. They are as follows:

Welala Assefa[11] is 58 years old.[12] She has had no formal training as an actress, but has worked for the City Hall Theatre for 39 years. Welala is a much loved popular actress in Ethiopia, who in recent years has been able to build on her theatrical reputation by taking a role in a prominent television soap opera and acting in numerous films. At the time of writing she was in rehearsal for a new production to open shortly at City Hall.

Elizabeth Melaku is 50 years old. She was one of the first graduates from the Theatre Arts Department at Addis Ababa University and has worked as an actress for 25 years. She is a highly regarded, famous and popular actress who has played a wide range of leading roles. Elizabeth worked for the state theatres until 2010 when she decided to turn freelance. However, this decision left her in a precarious financial position and so she recently accepted a relatively poorly paid position as stage manager at the state Children's Theatre. Alone of the actresses interviewed, Elizabeth has been very reluctant to work in film, although her debut role in *Lomi Shita* (*Scent of a Lemon*) won her the award of Best Actress at the all-Africa Nile Film Festival of 2012. At the time of interview she was starring in a privately produced play, *Keselamet Gare* (*With Greetings*), put on at the Empress Taytu Hotel. She is interested in exploring the possibilities of writing and directing plays.

Hiwot Arrage is 40 years old. She gained a Theatre Arts degree in 2008, but has been working as an actress for 17 years. For many years Hiwot was a full-time actress at the Hagar Fikir, but she now works regularly on radio and TV and in film. She is also employed in the government Culture and Tourism Office as a senior officer for cultural promotion. When interviewed she was back at the Hager Fikir as a guest actress and also rehearsing for a role in a play at the City Hall Theatre. Like many older actresses she has tended to be typecast. Her whole career has almost exclusively involved playing someone's mother.

Bayushe Alemayhu is 38 years old. She was not formally trained but has worked in theatre for 15 years. She is a full time actress at the Hagar Fikir, and when interviewed was acting concurrently in two plays there, including the lead role in a romance, *Yegude Ken* (*The Day of Bad Secrets*) by Hiwot Abeje.

Etaferawe Meberatu is 30 years old. Like Hiwot she graduated in Theatre Arts in 2008. She immediately secured a permanent job at the National Theatre and has worked there ever since. Etaferawe rose to fame through her performance as an Ethiopan queen in the play *Hendake* (*Queen Mother*) by Malkamu Zerihun, which was a triumph for both theatre and actress. She is currently acting in two plays running in repertory at the National, and has had roles in three recent films.

Adisalem Merga is 25 years old and has been acting for 11 years, although she only gained her degree in 2011. She has no permanent job but has had two recent roles as a guest actress at the Hagar Fikir and at the time of interview was in rehearsal for another part at the same theatre. She is currently less famous than the other actresses interviewed, but is beginning to gain a strong reputation.

Becoming an actress

Most of the actresses interviewed said that they were initially drawn into theatre by involvement with drama either in school or at a club. Our youngest interviewee, Adisalem Merga, acted in her high school, and for Red Cross and HIV awareness raising clubs in her home town of Debre Zeit (some 40 kilometres from Addis Ababa) before choosing to study theatre at university. Bayushe Alemayhu and Hiwot Arrage became involved in semi-professional theatre clubs as teenagers, which involved them from a young age in theatre tours. Elizabeth Melaku first got involved through school plays but was also taken to the theatre by her mother as a child, and Etaferawe Meberatu said she always dreamed of being an actress and went to shows whenever she could. Only Welala Assefa had no idea of acting as a child:

> I dreamt of being a singer, but at that time I failed the exam I took to be a singer at the Hagar Fikir Theatre. I waited for another announcement, and finally I heard there is a call for traditional dancers at the Municipality Theatre [also known as the City Hall]. I thought this would be the best way and opportunity to become a singer over time. I went to City Hall for the entrance exam but they had finished registration for dancers. However, they told me that if I wanted to be an actress they had not finished registering for the exam. Because I had no choice I registered and they gave me a monologue by Empress Tewabach for exam preparation. I passed the exam.

Social attitudes: families and husbands

Welala was able to pursue her desire for a life on stage only because both her parents were dead. She says that in her professional lifetime social acceptance of actresses has improved enormously:

> In this generation things are very easy for actresses. I feel sorry for those [of her own generation] who really wanted to be an actress, but they couldn't face the challenge of their family members and society. This is the reason why I see myself as a lucky person; because those bad days have passed. [...] Now I receive much respect and love from society [...] but when I was young theatre was seen as shameful work. Society saw us as bad mannered, and actresses as people not fit to marry. They were considered to be people who couldn't stay at home and be loyal to a husband, but would easily be

persuaded to sleep with anyone. [...] They considered anyone working as an actress as trash.

Although it is undoubtedly true that social acceptance of actresses is much improved this is a fairly recent change. Most of the families of the women we talked to were reluctant to see their daughters take to the professional stage. Even now, conservative perceptions of women's roles, and fears about how girls will be treated, vie with an increasing urban recognition that educated women want a professional life and the glamour, fame and perceived income generating potential of leading performers.

Of the actresses interviewed only Welala and Elizabeth encountered no resistance when they said they wanted to go on stage. All the others were forced at times to deceive or confront their families. Adisalem had been told to register for a degree in marketing, but secretly put her name down for a theatre course in the evenings. Hiwot pretended she was attending a typing class when she was actually at a theatre club. Bayushe was brought up by her grandmother, who hoped her granddaughter would work in an office and marry young. She also secretly attended a semi-professional theatre club, but could no longer conceal what she had been doing when the group was to take a play on tour. When she finally confessed, and said she wanted to travel with the club, her grandmother said that if she chose to go she could never return home. Bayushe went. Etaferawe's family had been very supportive of her interest in drama as a child, giving her money to go to theatre and enjoying her acting out various roles at home. However, she also defied her family to take part in a theatre club. She says: 'They didn't believe this profession could be a lifetime career until they saw I graduated with a BA and got work as a permanent employee in the government sector [at the National Theatre].'

If parents and grandparents are dubious about acting as a profession for women, husbands seem even more conflicted. Some interviewees were understandably protective of their marriages and reticent about any strains caused by the very public nature of their work, by male jealousy, and by the extraordinary levels of abuse some men's family and friends feel free to pour on actress-wives. Hiwot had few reservations about speaking openly. She said that her husband sometimes becomes worried and jealous, partly because he feels belittled when he is out with her in public and her admirers want to speak to her while ignoring him, but more importantly because his family and friends openly question her sexual fidelity. Particularly critical of Amhara patriarchal culture, Hiwot says that, even when a couple love each other, cultural expectations of gender roles are such that it is difficult for marriages which involve a woman on stage not to end in divorce. She gave the example of being interviewed for this article on the eve of the national New Year holiday: 'Right now, what would be more comfortable for him? For me to be at home, or at this interview? It is obvious. Always men need to have women under their influence and control; to show them that they are better.' She refers to Ethiopian men as *abesh wend*, meaning that all are equally oppressive, seeing women as inherently liable to behave dishonourably and wanting wives to be entirely dependent on their men. If Hiwot is particularly caustic about gender relations within marriage for actresses, Bayushe independently backed up her assertions about how husbands' friends and family insult actresses. She says that people have sometimes asked her in public why and how her husband married her, saying they would never marry an actress because they would not trust her or believe she could be loyal to one man. Adisalem spoke in a similar manner. She says her engineer husband does trust her, but that his associates find this incredible, and that society refers to actresses as *dureya*: people who are vulgar or of easy virtue. Even Etaferawe, who says her husband is proud of her and likes to boast that he has a famous actress for a wife, acknowledges that many theatrical marriages are not stable. She also told us that it is difficult for actresses to choose a good husband, not because they lack proposals, but because it is hard for them to know if they are really loved, or if the men just want the kudos of a glamorous and famous wife.

Of the women we spoke to, only Elizabeth is unmarried, and she has made a considered decision to remain single:

> I am not free at weekends; that is working time. And even when I come home it is work time and I need time and concentration. I couldn't be there for social duties. [...] Much as I would like someone for a lovely friendship, most of the time men don't like my professional work. So it is my choice: either drop the job or drop the proposed husband. I know what kind of opportunities I have missed for the sake of my profession.

Working as an actress in Ethiopia

Ethiopian actresses are unusually fortunate, compared with African actresses elsewhere, in that those hired as permanent company members of the state theatres have secure employment. Moreover this employment does not preclude them from taking on other work as long as it does not interfere with their primary job. Companies like the National have a huge number of employees, many of whom are under-employed. Etaferawe told us that she was not given an acting part until she had been employed for two years, and that she had taken on a number of film and TV roles outside of her regular job.

However, wages are not high. A reasonably experienced actress without a degree earns around 1,500 birr (less than US$ 40) per month. An actress with a degree is paid 2,500 birr, which is why Hiwot Arrrage undertook an extension course after years of professional practice, and why Bayushe has recently also registered for a part time qualification. Addis Ababa is an expensive city to live in, and actresses are not high on government pay scales. Even a junior academic, for example, could expect to earn twice as much.

In response to long term discontent the state theatres recently introduced an incentive scheme through which workers share a proportion of the profits. Elizabeth expressed the widespread derision for the value of the scheme: 'There is no overtime payment, but every show has its own incentives. These are 10% of the general income of the theatre and this is divided between all crew members, actors and actresses. Sometimes this incentive would be [worth] only 10 birr per month. So it is better not to think that there is a payment.'

Moreover, although theatres are supposed to provide actors with all necessary costumes, make-up and so on, this seems to be the exception rather than the rule. Bayushe explains: 'If I ask for six costumes and three pairs of shoes I will probably get two costumes and one pair of shoes. [...] The main problem is that the management have no experience of what the whole process of being an actress means. [...] For them there is no way to adapt government policies to our professional needs. They just try to interpret policy as though this was any ordinary governmental work.'

Guest actors and those working for private companies have a different pay structure. A junior at the National Theatre can earn as little as 50 birr per performance, although this rises to 500 birr for a leading actress, and up to 600 birr in a private company. Working in theatre, unsupplemented by TV and film work, is certainly no way to become wealthy. Several interviewees commented on the mismatch between levels of celebrity and lifestyle. None of the actresses we interviewed has their own car, and the struggle to get a place on the minibuses which provide most of Addis Ababa's public transport after an evening show is a particular source of stress:

> Etaferawe: At night, after I have finished a performance, I have to struggle to get a seat in a taxi, and fight for a place with audience members who a minute ago saw me as an Ethiopian queen. This shames me in front of my fans and makes me feel bad. Most audience members think I am weird and some ask me why I am there.

> Bayushe: Society loves, admires and respects me very much. [...] But when people see me in the struggle to get a taxi they are amazed. And also they harass me when they see me in the chip shop buying a potato.

The wage issue of course affects both actors and actresses, but while a tiny number of women playwrights, directors and theatre executives exist, and despite a range of pro-women government policies, the common consensus among the actresses we spoke to was that there is a glass ceiling beyond which it is extremely hard for women to advance. Etaferawe says the positive discrimination policies are just propaganda: 'When it comes to reality, the dominance of men is still seen. They don't believe women can do anything like directing, managing or writing independently.' It is not that actors do not move into other roles but, as Elizabeth explained: 'When opportunities have been announced to become a director, or for another top position, almost always they are taken by men'. Hiwot Arrage goes so far as to argue that men actively put obstacles in the way of women's promotion: 'because if she gets a position as manager or director the men will be furious. They are not ready to be subordinate to women.' Hiwot also says that men are particularly nervous of educated women. However, it is important to note that Elizabeth saw the problem as being more complex than the denial of opportunities for women: she believes that women also internalize their inferiority. 'Most of the actresses don't want to act, and also they don't believe that they could direct plays.'

A final source of traumatic stress is that some (by no means all) directors still expect that actresses, particularly younger actresses, will be available for sex. Notably, our youngest actress, Adisalem Merga, still making her way in the profession, had most to say on this subject: 'They will give me a script, and the next day when I go for rehearsal there is no rehearsal but the director's or the producer's hands will be all over my body, touching me. They don't hesitate to ask for sex, and when I refuse they say: "I'm not asking you to marry me, just to make love for one day. What is your problem?"'

Both Adisalem and Hiwot say this is an even bigger problem in the film industry where many of the young women involved are not professional actresses, but amateurs and models seeking fame, and therefore particularly vulnerable to abuse from powerful men. Adisalem told us: 'They come to work because the director wants to sleep with them.'

As well as the sexual difficulties and inequality of opportunity they faced, we were also interested in Ethiopian actresses's experiences of the process of working on a play. Happily things have improved since the earliest plays were performed a century ago, when playwright-directors were seen as all powerful and actors merely as tools for delivering the text. However, the extreme status divide persisted for longer than one might have thought. Actors have only really begun to be seen as partners in the process of play-making since theatre became an area of university study, and even now many older directors display decidedly dictatorial attitudes.[13] Although acting and directing are taught at the University, the teachers are not specialists, and few have first-hand experience of any theatre outside Ethiopia.[14] Indeed, Ethiopian theatre is markedly different in style from any other I have encountered. Some productions, perhaps most notably those directed by Manyazewal Endeshaw, have experimented with modernist theatre forms (expressionism and absurdism) but these have never been widely appreciated. Under the Marxist Derg rule of 1974–1991 Soviet-style agitprop was a great influence. However, the most tenacious influence is that of the Ethiopian Orthodox Church, according to which characters are often viewed as symbolic types, with heroes acting in a grand, portentious manner while 'light' characters are often portrayed as fools rushing around without dignity. Even staging is influenced by the iconography of the Church, with dark, rich colours and monolithic sets for heroic tragedy, and light, bright colours for comedy. Characters tend to be viewed as types, so characterization is seldom well developed in rehearsal, and directors often focus their attention on line learning and blocking.

Few of our interviewees gave many details of their experiences of working on plays. There seems to be a general recognition that directors' skill levels vary considerably, and several interviewees said they thought the younger directors, trained at the University, had more skills than their elders.[15] There were also a number of accusations of favouritism among directors. Very little was offered about how the actress herself contributed to the process of rehearsal. By far the most thoughtful respondent on this subject was Elizabeth Melaku. Elizabeth is well known as a leading actress and says she is usually given psychologically complex roles. She discussed at some length different directing styles, although she was circumspect in her comments and said she tries not to cause trouble even if she is cast in a play she finds unconvincing: 'because if I drop out of their work of art, the director or writer would consider I had disgraced them, and never cast me again.'

Elizabeth spoke of Abate Mekuria as an example of a leading director who leaps straight into lines, blocking and characterization all at the same time, with everyone on stage from the beginning of the rehearsal process, and she said that he never even came to see a show once it had opened. She also spoke (without giving names) of 'irresponsible directors': 'When I am working with this kind of director, actors and actresses direct the play together. They try to catch the intention of the director and writer. Even though this is not the right way, it is the only solution to save the performance and your reputation in front of the fans.'

By contrast, Elizabeth discussed the preparation process in the two plays she directed with Alazare Samuel and also of working with Manyazawel Endeshaw. Here she says preliminary time was given to reading, speech patterns and discussions about emotions, before work began on blocking. She is also appreciative of how Alazare Samuel returns to rehearsals after the opening night to build on the responses from actors and audiences.

Finally, several actresses complained about the representation of women in Ethiopian theatre. This problem was widely linked to the fact that the great majority of playwrights are men. Elizabeth explained that the central role in any play was usually male and that female characters are normally secondary: objects elucidating aspects of the male hero's life, rather than the subject of the drama.

Why be an actress?

In all the interviews it was evident that, while their situation had markedly improved over the last 30 years, Ethiopian actresses remain objects of suspicion, regularly subjected to sexual abuse and social marginalization, and that this causes them significant distress. So why would a woman choose acting as a career?

Undoubtedly, one positive factor is the allure of fame, glamour and the love of a host of fans. The younger actresses put great emphasis on glamour. Adisalem sees her work as full of 'possibilities and opportunities in Ethiopia to become popular and rich'. Etaferawe insists that 'most of the people love, appreciate and encourage me. [...] Most of my fans are my friends on Facebook.' Bayushe is more cautious: 'Being an actress is not a simple task in Ethiopia. It demands much commitment, courage and sacrifice.' But she also explains the lure of fame: 'Once you are addicted to hearing the fans' applause, you will never want to return to your old life.' It was significant that several actresses emphasized the 'love and respect' they got from fans. The word 'respect' (used by Walela, Bayushe and Elizabeth) is particularly interesting in the light of the accounts of personal abuse and disrespect we were told. Clearly, the validation of their chosen profession by an adoring fan base is extremely important and sustaining to these actresses.

A personal love of acting and working in the theatre must also be taken into consideration. Etaferawe expressed this clearly: 'When I perform on stage my life has meaning, happiness and satisfaction.' Elizabeth Melaku feels similarly about her work: 'Personally I love the profession, and most of the people love it.' Even Hiwot, who in her interview was the most negative about the lot of Ethiopian actresses, is compelled by a real love for her work: theatre, she says, is 'work for the sake of love and passion. In this way you can be satisfied and fulfil your dream.'

It is evident that the position of Ethiopian actresses has radically transformed in many ways since comparable research was undertaken in the 1980s. Many families now support their daughters' choice to go on stage, hoping that acting, particularly on TV and for film, will lead to fame and fortune. Leading actresses are famous and attract fans, just like celebrities the world over. However, for many, theatre and acting is a vocation rather than a sensible or lucrative choice. Although the glamour of being a leading actress may equate to that of celebrity in the West, the pay and conditions certainly do not. Moreover the sexism and patriarchy of Amhara culture appears to be alive and well. Contemporary actresses may be able to find husbands more easily than was possible thirty years ago, but the appalling abuse and slander many routinely endure from the supposed friends and family of these men undercut any notion that government policies in support of gender equality have yet had much effect in changing social attitudes to actresses. It is not easy in Ethiopia, even today, for women to discuss their gendered oppression openly, and we close this article by thanking our interviewees for their courage in speaking to us so candidly about their lives both in and out of theatre.

NOTES

1 All interviews were conducted in Amharic and translated by Mahlet Solomon.
2 Although in the West it is often considered sexist not to refer to both genders as 'actors', this is not the case anywhere JP has worked in Africa, where the term 'actress' is always used for a female performer. This article therefore retains African usage.
3 The first Ethiopian play was *Fabula: Yawreoch Commedia (Fable: The Comedy of Animals)* by Teklehawariat Teklemariam. For more on the play see Berhanu & Solomon 2014. For an English language version of the play see Belayneh Abune (trans.) (2010).
4 For the early history of Ethiopian theatre see Plastow 1996: 103-105.
5 *Ibid*. 146-63.
6 *Ibid*. 207-14. My own involvement in Ethiopian theatre is due to the creation of the Theatre Arts Department. When it was established there were no Ethiopian theatre graduates so for the first few years a number of expatriate teachers were employed. I taught in the Department between 1984 and 1986. (JP)
7 See Ashegrie 2012.
8 *Ibid*. 2. In 1992 Aboneh Ashegrie interviewed Awlachew Dejene, who played female parts but refused to discuss his experiences, saying: 'I don't want to remember and talk about the bitter and unpleasant side of my life.'
9 Plastow 1996: 211.
10 See http://www.ethioscoop.com/biography/3479-azeb-worku-sibane.html, accessed 29.12.2014.
11 In Ethiopia there is no such thing as a family name. People are commonly referred to by their given (first) name. The second name is the given name of one's father. In this article actresses are therefore referred to by their first names.
12 All ages are given as of the time of interview, in late 2014.
13 In 2013 I returned to Ethiopia, after a decade away, to teach intensively on a new MA in Theatre at Addis Ababa University. My oldest student was a well-known director, who had been my undergraduate student in the 1980s. We were studying community-based theatre, but even in this role, whenever the man was given a small directing exercise he immediately resorted to shouting at actors and behaving in a dictatorial manner. When challenged he asserted that in his experience actors were lazy and this was the only way to make them perform. When he was later given very poor grades for his practical work he protested vehemently, apparently unable to see that his approach was antipathetic to making theatre with or for community groups. (JP)
14 Manyazawel Endeshaw gained an MA in theatre in Germany in the 1990s; veteran playwright, theatre owner and director Ayalneh Mulat studied journalism in Russia; neither of them currently teaches at the University. Indeed none of the contemporary teaching staff has a higher degree than a BA, in each case from the University of Addis Ababa, so new theatrical ideas are slow to penetrate in Ethiopia.
15 Most older directors became prominent during a time when theatre was more hierarchical than it is now. Until the 1980s playwrights were greatly honoured, and usually directed their own plays. Actors, on the other hand, were seen as mere puppets, employed to do as they were told. This led to very dictatorial directing styles. Younger directors, most of whom studied alongside those who are now their actors, tend to both have more egalitarian ideas, and cannot so easily pull rank on performers.

REFERENCES

Abune, Belayneh (trans.) (2010) in Hutchison, Yvette (ed.) *African Theatre 9: Histories: 1850–1950* (Oxford: James Currey), 153-67.
Ashegrie, Aboneh (2012) 'The Role of Women on the Ethiopian Stage', *Journal of African Cultural Studies*, 24, 1: 1-8.

Berhanu, Lealem & Mahlet Solomon (2014) 'Religious and Social Influences on the First Ethiopian Playwright, Teklehawariat Teklemariam, and his play *Fabula Yawreoch Commedia*', *Journal of African Studies*, 26, 3: 276–86.

Plastow, Jane (1996) *African Theatre and Politics: The evolution of theatre in Ethiopia, Tanzania and Zimbabwe* (Amsterdam: Rodopi).

Introducing *The Sentence* by Sefi Atta

CHRISTINE MATZKE

In October 2011 the Theater Krefeld/Mönchengladbach, Germany, staged the overall world premiere of Sefi Atta's play *The Sentence* in a German translation.[1] Drawing on judicial sentences of death by stoning in northern Nigeria in the early 2000s, *The Sentence* recounts the story of a Muslim woman unjustly sentenced to death for adultery. As the play progresses the protagonist not only becomes a symbol of injustice in the Nigerian and international media. It also transpires that she has been interpellated,[2] and actively participates in a system based on gender inequality and religious bigotry. Atta adapted the play from a short story, 'Hailstones on Zamfara', which was initially conceived as a monologue and later published in her collection of short stories, *Lawless and Other Stories* (2008) (US/UK edition: *News from Home* (2010)). In 2011 Salzburg-based Nigerian director Nicholas Monu directed the play at Krefeld/Mönchengladbach as part of their 'non-European theatre' programme. The series had been initiated by the director of drama, Matthias Gehrt, in 2010 to stage productions other than the common staples of German municipal theatres (*Stadttheater*) – Northern classics, comedy and increasingly musicals – by introducing one new non-European drama per season (Matzke 2013). Each play was to be translated into German and performed by the Krefeld/Mönchengladbach company, but directed by someone closer to its dramatic context: hence the choice of Monu to direct Atta.[3] Monu was familiar with Atta's work and had already directed another of her plays, *The Cost of Living*, at Terra Kulture in Lagos earlier that year.

Atta herself is a US-based Nigerian, best known as a novelist and writer of short stories. She is the author of *Everything Good Will Come* (2005) for which she received the first Wole Soyinka Prize for Literature in Africa in 2006, *Swallow* (2010) and her more recent *A Bit of a Difference* (2013). Little is known of her dramatic work for radio, stage and screen, even though, according to a recent interview, she prefers writing plays to any other genre (Geosi Reads 2013). To date, Atta has five stage plays to her credit, none of them published, but all of them produced (http://www.sefiatta.com/plays.html).

The monologue on which *The Sentence* is based was Atta's direct response to the news of Safiya Hussaini's and Amina Lawal's sentences to death by stoning for adultery in northern Nigeria,[4] in December 2001 and March 2002 respectively (Vöhringer 2011), shortly after 9/11. The play is set in the northern Nigerian state of Zamfara, around the time of the introduction of shari'a law in October 1999. It does *not* address the events of 9/11 and should not be seen as belonging to what has been labelled the 'post-9/11 genre' (Mohr & Mayer 2010: 3) but 9/11 nonetheless haunts the text, Atta being based in the United States, and also writing under her birth name. In an autobiographical essay entitled 'One or the Other' she writes: 'After September 11, Atta became one of the most hated names in the United States (on account of Mohammad Atta) and Gboyega [Sefi Atta's husband] jokingly suggested that I might want to reconsider my pen name. I told him I would stick with Sefi Atta and live with the consequences' (2008).

In the same essay, and in a questionnaire returned to Manfred Vöhringer, the Krefeld/Mönchengladbach dramaturge, Atta also refers to her family history to contextualize the play, particularly the life of her paternal grandfather, Ibrahim Atta (1884-1964), the Ohinoyi of Ebiraland from 1917 to 1954, who is widely acknowledged as a far-sighted, innovative ruler with great appreciation for community progress and education (Kashim & Abdullah 2013). In the above questionnaire (Vöhringer 2011) she notes:

> I wrote *The Sentence* to record my response to the news of Amina Lawal's and Safiya Hussaini's sentences. Like many Nigerians, I felt they were draconian sentences, but had I not read my grandfather's memoir,[5] I may never have known how retrogressive they were in the context of Nigeria's history, which was forgotten in the international furore that followed.

In Atta's view, northern Nigeria was more broadminded and progressive in her grandfather's time than in the early twenty-first century, and this informed her writing of the play. What readers and viewers therefore encounter in the text are multiple layers of recent Nigerian history and Islamic practice, which do not follow the well trodden 'limited ways', to quote Peter Morey and Amina Yaqin, in which 'Muslims are stereotyped and "framed" within the political, cultural and media discourse of the West' (2011: 2). Instead, *The Sentence* defies any one-dimensional reading by remaining ambiguous on a number of the issues addressed: religious fundamentalism, gender dynamics and imagined global sisterhood, perceptions of justice and violence, questions of class, access to socio-political power, and the role of both national and international media. I close with the author's comment on the play as the frame through which we are encouraged to engage with *The Sentence*:

> I am reluctant to define it [the play] in a way that might limit how people interpret it. Whether or not the sentence is religiously motivated is subject to discussion, but we must also consider the political and cultural climate in which the characters exist. What I will say is that religious fundamentalism, patriarchy and autocracy are

connected and they seldom exist separately. Combined, they consistently result in the oppression of women. [...]
   Contradiction is a necessary element of storytelling that is grounded in reality. I toy with the idea of power throughout this play. It is essentially a play about power play. [The protagonist's] husband is weak, yet abusive towards her. At the same time, he is a victim of stringent state laws. She is strong, yet she is a victim of his abuse. In turn, she is a victimizer, to the extent that she mistreats his junior wife. I don't write about women who are nothing but victims or men who are nothing but abusers because I have not met any. (Vöhringer 2011)

AKNOWLEDGEMENTS

I wish to thank Sefi Atta and the Theater Krefeld/Mönchengladbach for generously sharing their time and sources with me.

NOTES

1   The German translation of *The Sentence*, 'Hagel auf Zamfara', translated by Eva Plorin, is available on request from Theatralize.Company, Munich, Germany (http://www.theatralize.com/).
2   Here, 'interpellated' is used in the Althusserian sense as 'hailed' by the 'ideology' of the system (Althusser 1971: 162).
3   Unfortunately, the production details and the German reception of the play are beyond the scope of this introduction. I deal with these issues in a forthcoming article provisionally entitled 'Staging Islam: Sefi Atta's *Hagel auf Zamfara* (*The Sentence*) at the Theater Krefeld/ Mönchengladbach'.
4   It should be noted that neither of the sentences was actually carried out.
5   Ibrahim Atta's memoir is partly reprinted in Sefi Atta's essay 'One or the Other'. In Europe, the full memoir is available in A.O. Ozigi's *Life and Times of a Visionary Ruler: A biography of Alhaji Ibrahim Onoruoiza Atta of Ebiraland* [2007] at Oxford University Library. Ozigi is not available through interlibrary loan, and it is also out of print; I am relying on Sefi Atta's rendering of Ibrahim Atta. Sefi Atta herself grew up in a multi-religious environment, her father being a Muslim, her mother a Christian. Today she no longer practises any religion ('One or the Other').

REFERENCES

Althusser, Louis (1971) 'Ideology and Ideological State Apparatuses (Notes towards and Investigation) [April 1970]', in *Lenin and Philosophy and Other Essays*, trans. Ben Brewster (London: New Left Books), 121-73.
Atta, Sefi (2005) *Everything Good Will Come: A Novel* (Northampton, MA: Interlink Books).
—— (2008) *Swallow: A novel* (Lagos: Farafina).
—— (2008) 'One or the Other', available at: http://www.africanwriter.com/one-or-the-other-by-sefi-atta/, accessed 10 May 2013.
—— (2010) *News from Home: Stories* (Northampton, MA: Interlink Books), 15-36; initially published in 2008 as *Lawless and Other Stories* (Lagos: Farafina).
—— (2013) *A Bit of Difference* (Northampton, MA: Interlink Books).
—— http://www.sefiatta.com/index.html, accessed 15 November 2014.

Geosi Reads (2012) 'Interview with Sefi Atta', available at: http://geosireads.wordpress.com/2013/02/27/interview-with-nigerian-writer-sefi-atta/, accessed 14 November 2014.

Kashim, Usman & Binta Ahmed Abdullah (2013) 'Nigeria: Ibrahim Atta – Remembering the Ohinoyi of Ebiraland (1884-1964)', *Daily Trust*, 8 March, available at: allafrica.com/stories/201303090226-html, accessed 23 April 2014.

Matzke, Christine (2013) unpublished telephone interview with Manfred Vöhringer on 10 May 2013.

Mohr, Dunja M. and Sylvia Mayer (2010) 'Introduction: 9/11 as Catalyst – American and British Cultural Responses', *Zeitschrift für Anglistik und Amerikanistik*, 58, 1: 1-4.

Monu, Nick (2013) unpublished email to the author, 27 May.

Morey, Peter, and Amina Yaqin (2011) *Framing Muslims: Stereotyping and Representation after 9/11* (London: Harvard University Press).

Vöhringer, Manfred (2011) unpublished email questionnaire/interview with Sefi Atta, July.

—— (Season 2011/2012/2013) 'Machtfragen: Sefi Atta im Gespräch', trans. Leona Benneker, *Hagel auf Zamfara von Sefi Atta, Uraufführung*, Programme, Issue 39 (Theater Krefeld/Mönchengladbach), 6-8 (German translation of parts of the above interview).

The Sentence
Sefi Atta

SUMMARY

The Sentence is adapted from 'Hailstones on Zamfara,' which was initially written as a monologue and later published as a short story. *The Sentence* presents the story in its original form, a play about religious hypocrisy and fundamentalism, in which an unnamed Moslem woman recounts how she was wrongfully sentenced to death for adultery.

CHARACTERS
Woman
Husband
Junior Wife
Imaginary Man
Miriam Maliki

It is possible to have only three actors in this play. The roles of Husband and Imaginary Man, Junior Wife and Miriam Maliki can be doubled up.

SETTING
A prison cell

SCENE 1

*A **Woman** sits on a stool by a bucket. She is dressed in black traditional Moslem wear. She carries white prayer beads. By her feet are mangoes.*

Woman On the day I die I will arise, and my executioners will finally be forced to admit, 'We were wrong. We should have revered you more'. I am not guilty. I have always preferred men as I make them up in my head; imaginary men. Not the kind some women want, those silly fantasy men in romance books. My men are plain – ugly, even – with facial marks, oily skins, dust in their hair. They ride motorcycles, take buses and taxis to their places of work. They walk mostly. They never own cars, otherwise they would have to be rich men, the kind

who become senators, chairmen of banks and such. No, my men have spread-out feet from being barefoot as children. They have palms as brown as tobacco leaves. Some have had a hand cut off because they stole to eat. Still, they pray as good Moslems should, five times a day.
Enter **Husband**.

Woman Did my husband think I was pretending the day I stopped hearing him? Had he forgotten he caused the very condition that made him so angry? I tried to help him understand.
    'You call me, I can't hear. You insult me, I can't hear. You tell me to get out of your house. How can I leave when I can't hear?'

Husband You witch! I know you're doing this on purpose!

Woman It is not my fault. My left ear is damaged from the beating you gave me. Sometimes I hear, sometimes I don't, even if I face Mecca.

Husband I divorce thee!

Woman Huh?

Husband I divorce thee!

Woman You must be asking for food again. I'm off to the market.

Exit **Husband**.

Woman Where else would I go so early that morning? The trouble with my husband was that his anger was like lightning. Lightning from drinking too much *burukutu*, wasting half the profits from his mechanic's shop, and not being accountable for his actions afterwards. Lightning loves to show off. 'Look at me. See what I do with the night? Let me turn it to day and confuse you'. I came home one day, and he would be calm. I came home the next, and he behaved as though I'd insulted his father's lineage. Off and on, that was my husband, like lightning before thunder comes along and shows who is in control.

Enter **Junior Wife**. *She is a shy, teenage bride.*

Woman He was angry that day because I was not enthusiastic about his announced betrothal, so he boxed my ears. I showed him thunder – the thunder of no secondary education; of being married to him at fourteen; motherhood three times over. To prove my endurance, I even chaperoned his new bride, a girl the same age as my eldest daughter, Fatima. I called her 'Junior Wife', and from then on called him 'Our Husband'.

SCENE 2

Woman Junior Wife came to me the morning after her wedding night.

Junior Wife *cries*.

Woman She made me so angry. I had raised mine already. I did not want another child around the house.

Junior Wife It pains me.

Woman It will eventually stop.

Junior Wife I want to go home.

Woman You're lazy. You did not rise early to make Our Husband's tea. You're supposed to make his tea from now on.

Junior Wife You see me crying. You don't even take pity on me. At least you are old. You should be like a mother to me.

Woman I'm thirty-two years old.

Junior Wife runs off stage crying.

Woman She ran home that first week.

Junior Wife returns with a bundle.

Woman But her father sent her back with a bundle of kola nuts to appease Our Husband. I asked my daughters not to play with her, Fatima, my eldest, especially. I told her gently, 'You're supposed to respect her. She is your father's new wife'. Fatima said, 'Then I should marry my father's friend, so that we can play'. I laughed. Fatima's mouth was too sharp. 'You're going to finish secondary school before you marry', I said. 'I will suffer anything for that right'.

Junior Wife cries again.

Woman Junior Wife cried. She said she had always dreamed of finishing secondary school; she was particularly good at multiplication.

She was always feeling sorry for herself, and if I was ever like that, I did not care to be reminded by her sad presence. I would be fair to her, I promised, so long as she performed her wifely duties and relieved me of mine. Then I gave her extra advice. 'Get fat as fast as I did, and he will surely marry someone else'. Our Husband was partial to bones; the bones of girls in particular.

SCENE 3

Woman Junior Wife came to me.

Junior Wife I'm pregnant.

Woman That's very good.

Junior Wife I vomited all morning.

Woman It's a girl, then.

Junior Wife Why?

Woman If it's a boy you would vomit all day.

Junior Wife I don't believe in that.

Woman Ask your mother. Didn't she teach you anything before you left?

Junior Wife It's not a girl. I know.

Woman I had not thought of that. I was so happy Our Husband left me alone at night I was lulled into a stupid state. I was even singing while I cooked. A boy? What would happen to the rest of Fatima's secondary education? I stared at Junior Wife's face. She had such a haughty expression. Pregnancy had made her stronger, as if she'd found a new companion I could not separate her from. She actually refused to bed Our Husband.

Junior Wife adopts an arrogant posture.

Junior Wife I have my limits. You were naive when this happened to you. You didn't know how to trick him. I've told him that if he touches me, his son will be miscarried instantly.

*Fig. 1: Woman
(Marianne Kittel) in
a performance of* The
Sentence *(Hagel auf
Zamfara) at the Theater
Mönchengladbach, 2013).*
(Photo © Matthias Stutte,
2013)

*Fig 2: Junior Wife (Helen
Wendt)*
(Photo © Matthias Stutte,
2013)

Woman He was dumb enough to swallow that fib? I wanted my hands to be busy. I did not want to hear about the possibility of a son. I should cook you a meal. To celebrate.

Junior Wife Many thanks, but I only eat what I myself have cooked from now on. My mother taught me that, at least.

Exit Junior Wife.

Woman What a cheek for her to assume I would be so malicious as to poison her.

As she grew bigger, the changes began in our town. The state government was building shari'a courts, appointing Alkalis to preside over them. That was the first time I heard that the Koran forbade women and men from travelling in the same buses, girls and boys from attending the same schools. Fatima and other final-year girls were transferred to an afternoon session. The boys had the morning sessions. By the afternoons, most teachers were tired and went home anyway, because the girl students were not many. Fatima's school marks remained high throughout. She even won a trip to a television station, after writing an essay about Heaven. She came back with her eyes so big: 'Mama, I met Miriam Maliki. She reads the news on television. She says I could train with the station after I leave school'.

I looked at my beautiful daughter, jumping up and down. Would anyone care what knowledge she had in her head? And if she ever were on television, how would I see her? 'We don't own a television', I said, to be the first to disappoint her. But she would not stop talking about her Miriam Maliki. Oh, Miriam Maliki had such a pretty smile. Oh, Miriam Maliki wore gold bangles and covered her hair to read the news, because her husband's family disapproved of her exposing herself. And oh, Miriam Maliki had been on Hajj to Mecca.

I thought, what a dimwit of a woman. To care about work when she came from a home with money. She could afford a trip to Mecca? And back? That was typical of the rich; nothing better to worry about. I thought I would tell her off, this Miriam Maliki, if ever I saw her. She had let women like me down.

Then before the end of school term Fatima's favourite teacher, her English teacher, was fined for braiding her hair with extensions. Allah – I don't tell a lie. The Alkali presiding over the poor woman's case warned her that she would spend time in jail if she didn't stop being fashionable. Hair perms were not allowed any more. Hair dye was not allowed, except dark brown and black. We heard of a thief in another town who had his hand cut off by a surgeon at the general hospital. The nurses there buried the hand instead of throwing it away. Our Husband came home complaining that people who drank *burukutu* were being flogged publicly.

We got word of the student in another school far from Fatima's. She too was to be flogged, because she was pregnant. Thirteen years old, and she said a man had raped her. Unfortunately, as she was a woman, her testimony was not greater than his.

SCENE 4
*Enter **Husband** in a drunken stupor.*
Woman Our Husband came to my room at night.
Husband It's your turn tonight.
*Husband grabs. **Woman** struggles.*
Woman It's not my turn! It's not my turn!

SCENE 5
***Woman** is distraught after her rape. Background sound of baby crying. Crying stops.*
Woman That was the night Junior Wife gave birth to a baby boy. Our Husband named him Abu. He announced that Abu was going to university and the rest of us would have to make sacrifices. I wandered around the whole day after Abu's naming ceremony, thinking of Fatima. I went to the tailor's to order a dress for her. I passed the Koranic lessons where young boys chanted verses. I stopped for cattle rearers. I smelled fresh blood in the abattoir. It made me sick. I heaved by the wood carvers' sheds and there he was. He had the facial marks of a peasant, my imaginary man.
*Enter **Imaginary Man** with a wooden bust of a woman. He has facial marks.*
Woman What happened to your hand?
Imaginary Man It got cut off.
Woman What did you do to get it cut off?
Imaginary Man I stole.
Woman Did you ask for penance?
Imaginary Man waves his stump.
Imaginary Man This is my penance.
Woman How do you carve?
Imaginary Man With my one arm.
Woman How do you pray?
Imaginary Man With my one arm.
Woman How do you love?
Imaginary Man points at his temple.
Imaginary Man Love is here.
Woman I'm a married woman.
Imaginary Man laughs.
Imaginary Man You have a sad face.
Woman Let me see your carving.
*Imaginary Man hands her the carving. **Woman** feels it in a suggestive manner.*
Imaginary Man I like you.
Woman What do you like about me?
Imaginary Man You remind me of my first cousin. I almost married her.
Imaginary Man watches as she continues to feel the carving.

Imaginary Man When did you become a bad woman?
Woman Today. I am not so well.
Woman stops and hands back the carving to him.
Woman What did you steal?
Imaginary Man A transistor radio.
Woman Why?
Imaginary Man I wanted to listen to the news.
Woman Why?
Imaginary Man I wanted to know what is going on in our town. I would have returned it. It was just a property dispute. Every sin in the world comes down to a property dispute.
Woman Not my husband's drinking. That is no property dispute.
Imaginary Man That, too. He drinks to appease himself. If a rich man drinks, who flogs him?
Woman It seems unreasonable to cut off a hand for stealing a transistor radio. For the sin of drinking, they really should cut a throat.
Imaginary Man You are a harsh woman.

SCENE 6
Woman I was pregnant by the end of that month. I had not been as sick as I normally was. I was sicker; sick all day. It made me thin. I was worrying about Fatima's schooling. I was running around for Junior Wife's newborn, Abu.
Background sound of baby crying. Crying stops.
Woman She was refusing to touch him. She said he might as well have been born a stone. She cursed her parents who gave her to Our Husband in exchange for a dowry. She said marriage was like slavery.

Everyone is quick to compare themselves to slaves. What slave had the power to tell Our Husband to let her sleep separately? I had to fake typhoid so that he would not come to me at night. My temperatures were easy; I was making his morning teas again. My nausea was convenient. Junior Wife told me one evening
Enter Junior Wife. She is tired from not sleeping.
Junior Wife You're hiding something from me. You seem one way while you are the other. You say one thing and mean the other. Our husband says you do this to drive people to madness.
Woman Have you fed your son?
Junior Wife See? You're doing it again.
Woman Your son needs to be fed.
Junior Wife My son is like you. A snake hidden in the grass. He does not cry so that I will worry about him. That is why I no longer sleep at night,
Woman He's an innocent child.
Junior Wife No, he isn't. His big head almost killed me.
*Background sound of baby crying. **Junior Wife** falls to the ground and rocks. **Woman** raises her voice to be heard.*

Woman By the end of the week she was rocking herself. Her baby was shrieking now, and it was I who was acting like his mother. *I*, who was carrying him and attending to his mess.

*Enter **Husband** angrily. He points at **Junior Wife**.*

Husband What is wrong with you?! Will you go and attend to your son for once?

Junior Wife gets up reluctantly.

Husband This household is cursed from top to bottom. One really has to be sure where one picks his brides. Everything is falling apart since she arrived. If she doesn't take heed, I will send her back to that father of hers.

Woman Threats. He was trying to outshriek his own son. What will happen to her baby then?

Husband He will stay here. My son will not be deserted. If his own mother won't care for him, I will accept the next best mother.

Woman Who?

Husband Who else? You, of course. And he will attend university. And he will become a doctor. And he will be rich. Then he can be president –

Woman Insha Allah. I'm sure he will, since he resembles you.

Husband Oh shut up.

*Baby stops crying and **Junior Wife** returns.*

Junior Wife Something terrible has come to pass. What?

Husband Have I married a couple of witches or what? Did I not just tell you to attend to your son?

Junior Wife Unfortunately he is dead.

Woman Who?

Junior Wife Abu.

Husband collapses.

SCENE 7

*Enter **Husband** cradling baby wrapped in white cloth.*

Woman I could have pitied him the way he mourned. He embalmed the body. He wrapped the body in white cloth. He dug a hole and placed it gently in. He covered the hole up. He even ordered a tombstone. One morning I heard him weeping like a woman.

Husband Abu! Abu!

Woman Would you like some tea?

Husband notices her and runs off in fright.

*Enter **Junior Wife** with a suitcase. She walks across stage.*

Woman That same week he sent Junior Wife packing, back to her father, because she had neglected his son. Neglected? But he was always dumb for her sad face. I was happy to see that murderer out of the house. To kill her own child; there was no excuse. I told Fatima when she started lamenting how two losses in one week were impossible to bear, 'Save your upsets. Save them for times that are worth it. They will come'.

*Enter **Husband** in a drunken stupor.*

Woman Our Husband was drinking *burukutu* like water now. He'd stopped going to work at his shop. He would leave home early in the mornings to do the work of drunkards. Meanwhile, his mechanics were pilfering from him. I thought, how did they dare in this new climate? That was some poverty. I would rather beg knowing I had two hands to show for myself.

Husband *dances in a drunken stupor.*

Woman We did not hear a word from Junior Wife who had returned to her father's house. We never even asked, so we did not know her father finally begged her forgiveness for abandoning her. He said he did it to make her strong, so that she would not be homesick and run away. She told him of Our Husband's drinking, and her father exclaimed, 'He drinks?'

Husband *suddenly stops dancing as if he is in shock.*

SCENE 8

Husband *lies face down, bracing himself.*

Woman They came for Our Husband while he was doing the work of drunkards. They took him to court. The Alkali presiding over his case ordered fifty strokes.

Husband *cries out three times as if he is being flogged.*

Woman I did not know any of this until his friends brought him home, whimpering like a baby. Fatima cried the most, of my daughters, as we lay him face down on his bed. He cursed Junior Wife and her father, and told me what happened.

Husband Let my sores fester! Leave me to die! Heaven awaits me!

Woman I've heard alcohol helps.

Husband You can't even say sorry.

Woman *begins to laugh hysterically.* **Husband** *is furious.*

Husband You evil woman. You will pay for this. You think it's funny? You will pay. Just wait. I will get better, and I will do something that will make you want to die.

Woman F-Fatima?

Husband W-what did Fatima ever do to me? It was you. Y-you and this horrible behaviour of yours since you lost your hearing. P-punishing me, punishing me, for what was m-merely an accident. Did you think I made you h-half deaf on purpose? C-curse you.

Woman So long as it was me.

SCENE 9

Husband *faces audience.*

Woman The day Our Husband was able to walk straight he went straight back to court and told them he had an accusation to make. The Alkali, knowing his face, asked him to make it concise.

Husband It is my wife. She is pregnant, by another man. She committed adultery and that is why I was drinking. My wife is a very loose woman.

Woman They came for me in the afternoon. What was I doing at the time? Dyeing my hair. My real hairs were so white. They told me of Our Husband's accusation in court. They took me into custody. I asked, 'Who will look after my children?' One of them answered, 'Why are you bothering to ask?'

That was when I met Miriam Maliki. She came to visit me in custody. I'll never forget the way she commanded the guards.

*Enter **Miriam Maliki** wearing a black scarf and gold bangles.*

Miriam Maliki Let her out of there. She's pregnant and she's no danger to anyone.

Woman Allah. In all my life, I'd not seen such a delicate woman with power, and she was as skinny as Junior Wife. I thought, this one, she hasn't suffered a second in her life.

Miriam Maliki I'm Miriam Maliki. Have you heard of me?

Woman My daughter said she met you.

Miriam Maliki Your daughter?

Woman Fatima.

Miriam Maliki Fat?

Woman Ima.

Miriam Malika What?

Woman That is her name. Fatima. You said you would train her, and she would be on the news. She was jumping up and down, and she even said –

Miriam Maliki Listen, it's you I'm worried about. Do you know I heard your story and immediately came out here? I could not believe what they were telling me. You were taken from your home? Like a mere criminal? To this mud dungeon with nothing but a bucket? And your own husband accused you? What did you tell them when they came for you?

Woman Who will look after my daughters?

Miriam Maliki Did you tell them you were innocent?

Woman Did they ask?

Miriam Maliki I'm sorry. I am so angry about this. Forgive me. I heard your trial is tomorrow. I'm disgusted by the prospects of such a case. I will be there at your side.

Woman My side?

Miriam Maliki Do not be afraid. Look at me. I know you're innocent. You will not be put to death.

Woman Death? For what?

Miriam Maliki Don't you know? Don't you know how these courts intend to punish married women who have committed adultery?

Woman How?

Miriam Maliki Death by stoning. Haven't you been following the news?

SCENE 10

Woman Indeed she was with me during my trial. Not by my side, but she was sitting with others who were allowed in the court. If she had been by my side, I might have been able to answer the questions better. 'Why didn't you tell your husband earlier that you were pregnant?' 'I just didn't'. 'How do you lie with a man who doesn't exist?' 'I just did'. Miriam came to spend time with me after my sentencing. She said all her life she never imagined this would happen in a place she lived, that a woman would be stoned to death for adultery. She said I was maligned, or raped. I told her imagination was a dangerous exploit.

Miriam Maliki You're brave. You're like a mountain.

Woman See me as I am instead.

Miriam Maliki paces.

Miriam Maliki The court was unfair to you. The state cannot sanction such courts. The federal government won't allow it. You know what this is really about?

Woman A property dispute?

Miriam Maliki What?

Woman I am going to die.

Miriam Maliki walks over and takes her hand.

Miriam Maliki I will make sure. I will so make sure people hear of you. Others have taken an interest, not just me. Elsewhere in the country they are writing about you in newspapers, calling this a barbaric injustice. Foreign papers are hearing about your case as we speak. Once they carry your story, there will be activists involved. They will petition our president. Very soon, our little court will be the focus of the world. You understand? It is very likely that your life will be saved because of this. Have hope. You are a symbol.

Miriam Maliki lets go of her hand.

Woman Fatima came to visit while Miriam was still with me. She brought me the mangoes. She told me her sisters were doing well, considering. She told me Our Husband was fasting and growing a beard for religious purposes. I told her, 'Tell your father Allah has his reward'. Was he allowing her to continue her secondary education nevertheless? She said he was. 'Make sure you get your education', I said. Make sure it's in your hands, then you can frame it and hang it on the wall, and when you go to your husband's house, carry it with you'.

'I don't think that's what education is', she said, 'something to hang on a wall'.

'Listen', I said, 'I know what I'm saying. What is in your head might not save you. Hang your education on the wall of your husband's house, so that whatever happens you can say to yourself, "This is my education", and no one can take it away from you'.

She left only after I ordered her. She wanted to stay, but I did not like her seeing me in custody. 'Did you include me in your essay of

Heaven?' I asked. She said no. I said, 'Therefore don't worry about me going there'.

Miriam Maliki Are you being sarcastic most times?

Woman Me?

Miriam Maliki I notice the way you talk. You say one thing and mean the other. I don't mean to be rude, but it's like I hardly know you.

Woman She hardly didn't.

Miriam Maliki Sometimes, I wonder if, forgive me, you are crazy. You and I, I feel for you so strongly, as though you matter more than my mother. Can I be bold? There is nothing to lose. I want to show you something.

Miriam Maliki unwraps her scarf and underneath her hair is dyed rainbow colours.

Woman It's prettier in the sky.

Miriam Maliki My husband says it's ugly. He says I've lost my head. He calls it my lost head, but he says it as a joke, mind you. I have two girls by him, you know. He loves them as boys. You will call me lucky to have such a man, but really, he should love them as girls. He also thinks he was my first. I married him when I was twenty-three, after I graduated from university. He was not my first. I lied that I was stretched by riding horses. I hope I'm not overwhelming you.

Woman A little. Why would she tell me now I was about to die? Would she tell me if I were not about to die?

Miriam Maliki What are you thinking?

Woman *looks at* **Miriam Maliki***'s bangles.*

Woman Are you rich?

Miriam Maliki attempts to hide her bangles.

Miriam Maliki Me? No. I am what you call comfortable. Why? Do you consider me...spoiled?

Woman Yes.

Miriam Maliki Are you scared to die?

Woman Yes.

Miriam Maliki begins to cry.

Miriam Maliki You're carrying a child. That will give you time. They will not stone you until your child is born.

Woman It's nothing.

Miriam Maliki Why didn't you answer the questions you were asked in court?

Woman I just didn't.

Miriam Maliki What really happened?

Woman What difference would it have made? (*To audience*) Our Husband's testimony, was greater than mine.

Miriam Maliki You shall not be forsaken.

Woman (*to audience*) In the name of Allah, the Beneficent, the Merciful.

THE END

Book reviews

Stephanie Newell & Onookome Okome (eds),
Popular Culture in Africa: The episteme of the everyday
New York & London: Routledge, Taylor & Francis, 2014
ISBN 9280415532921 (hbk) $140

Any book about popular culture in Africa is likely to find some orientation
from Karin Barber's seminal essays: 'Popular Arts in Africa' (1987) and
'Views from the Field' (1997). The editors of *Popular Culture in Africa* have
done more than touch base with these two important essays, they have
persuaded her to write a densely argued seven page Foreword in which she
revisits and sometimes corrects her earlier ideas. The editors' Introduction
reflects their allegiance to Barber's founding concepts, and almost every one
of the fifteen articles in the book cites Barber, usually in reverential mode.
The book is a Festschrift in all but name.

Barber's 'scholarly architecture', as Newell and Okome describe her
work, derives to some extent from Raymond Williams's categorization
of British culture into residual, dominant and emergent culture, which in
Barber's 1987 essay becomes transmuted into 'traditional, elite and popular',
although by 2014 she regrets this simplification, preferring to rely on more
complex, overlapping categories.

Much of the book is devoted to arguments about the tendency for
commentators to apply binary terminology, such as traditional/modern,
oral/literate and local/global. The various authors, anxious to deconstruct
false antinomies, emphasize simultaneous inclusion and exclusion. Barber
herself gives the example of Tanzanian Hip Hop, in which 'gangsta'
costumes seem to exclude the genre from mainstream society, while the
lyrics, for the most part, promote healthy lifestyles.

After the editors' Introduction *Popular Culture in Africa* is divided into
four parts: I Theoretical Overviews; II Gender and Sexuality; III The Place
of Humor; and IV Popular Discourses of the Streets.

The editors' overview is a very useful update of some arguments which emerged from Barber's earlier essays. Newell and Okome try to map the class and ethnic variables which are able to describe the literate, but to a large extent subaltern, groups who are most responsible for the creation of popular arts. These include 'sub-elites, emergent elites, local intellectuals, urban intellectuals, cultural brokers and local cosmopolitans'. The last term has given rise to a common colloquial construct: 'Afropolitan'.

The chapter also attempts to resolve some important conflicts between African Cultural Studies thinkers. One of these is: to what extent is innovation in popular culture the result of privatization and its stimulus to entrepreneurship, and to what extent are other external factors relevant, such as new media and the proletarianization of university graduates unable to find conventional jobs?

Another debate is between the terms 'popular culture' and 'popular art'. Barber preferred the latter because culture is too large, embracing non-aesthetic genres. The editors, however, have slightly deviated from Barber's practice by including a chapter by James Tsaiaor on football as a metaphor for the continuing European cultural and economic domination over Africa.

The second part of the essay tackles the subtitle of the book, *The episteme of the everyday*, with its echoes of Raymond Williams's dictum, 'Culture is Ordinary' (1989: 3-14). This shows how subaltern cultural studies can give popular audiences and readerships an insight into urban living, not available through elitist or canonical art forms. The chapter also references Achille Mbembe in struggling against another set of binaries: resistance/ passivity, autonomy/subjection, and civic society/state, with a similar plea for recognition of contradictions.

The first chapter in Part I, 'On Creativity in African Urban life: African cities as sites of creativity and emancipation', by Till Förster, concentrates on the history and analysis of urban Africa. He establishes some criteria which distinguish urban from rural living by describing the work on urbanization by late 19th- and early 20th-century sociologists, Georg Simmel and Louis Wirth, in order to unmask the causes and effects of European urbanization. Förster speculates that African cities show a similar tendency to innovation, which social diversity in big cities encourages. In particular he admires the recycling of urban detritus that African artists employ as a form of artistic 'recuperation' in such cities as Benin, Douala and Harare.

The second chapter in Part I, by Will Rea, is entitled 'Our Tradition is a very Modern Tradition: From cultural tradition to popular culture in southwestern Nigeria'. This is a fascinating account of the way a masquerade called Ẹgígún was 'invented' in Ìkọ̀lé at the beginning of the 20th century. Rea proceeds to trace the impact made by tradition, Christian modernization and secular modernism, and how all of these relate to shifting power traditions in Ìkọ̀lé In his conclusion Rea refers to the way multi-national donor groups such as the British Council, UNESCO and various NGOs are sometimes too influenced by northern cultural visions to realize the importance of hybrid forms of modern African art. This motif runs through other articles in the book.

In Uta Reuster-Jahn's Chapter 4 (the first in Part II), 'Sex and Relationship Education on the Streets', she explores advice given about love, sex and relationships in popular Swahili newspaper columns, pamphlets and romance fiction in Tanzania. Reuster-Jahn examines the claim by Tanzanian authors that their advice columns and didactic fiction fill a gap (created by cultural taboos) in young people's knowledge of sex and relationships. Despite the authors' claim to be supporting traditional values, ultimately the main drivers are commercial considerations.

Chapter 5, 'The Other Woman's Man is so Delicious' by Eiman Abbas H. El Nour, uses feminist analytical tools to understand the function of Sudanese women's songs which she traces from the late 19th century to the present time. Her conclusion is that the relative freedom women once had has been eroded to the point that they now display blatantly sexist attitudes by identifying the only respectable role in life for women as that of wife, even if it has to be in a bigamous relationship. El Nour believes that when women listen to these songs they tend to ignore the sexist lyrics and simply enjoy the rhythm of the music.

Chapters 6 and 8 both deal with the way in which colonial and neo-colonial influences have consolidated stereotypes of women. In '*Bingo*: Francophone African women and the rise of the glossy magazine', Tsitsi Jaji traces the history of a Senegalese magazine, *Bingo,* targeted at both sexes. Jaji follows the magazine from 1953 to 1965, from late colonialism to the first years of independence. Jaji spends much time deconstructing the neo-colonial adverts for Aspro, which through photographs and copy create an image of modern African women who keep Aspro as the medicine of choice for their families. Jaji contrasts these ersatz images with the realism of Sembene Ousmane's early film, *La Noire de...*

In Chapter 8, 'Desired State, Black Economic Empowerment and the South African Popular Romance', Christopher Warnes shows how a campaign called Black Economic Empowerment (BEE) promoted by the recently elected (1994) ANC dominant government had an impact on women's romance novels. One of the effects of BEE was to create a new class of upwardly mobile, mostly male entrepreneurs, some of whom became rich very quickly. This coincided with the creation of a romantic novel series published by Nollybooks and Saphire, which were aimed at women. The publishers laid down a template for the novels: a black female protagonist, after various pitfalls, finally manages to marry the wealthy target of her love. Warnes explains how an arguably progressive context, the rise of a post-Apartheid black middle class, was subverted by the neo-colonial formula, derived from Mills and Boon paperbacks, and the inevitable happy ending of the protagonist marrying her desired, wealthy, black husband.

Chapter 7, 'Better Ghana (Agenda)' does not fit well in the section on gender and sexuality. The author, Joseph Oduro-Frimpong, seems more interested in topical politics than in gender issues. This is confirmed by the chapter's subtitle: 'Akosua's political cartoons and critical public debates in contemporary Ghana'. The article is a well-observed study of cartoons by an artist with the pseudonym, Akosua, who criticizes a series of political leaders including heads of state.

The two chapters in Part III, The Place of Humor, are some of the most penetrating articles in the book. While the chapters in Part II dealt mainly with the defeat of African women (or their complicity in their own subjugation) those in Part III illustrate various methods of resistance to neo-colonialism, corruption or exploitation.

In Chapter 9, 'Stand up Comedy and the Ethics of Popular Performance in Nigeria', author Moradewun Adejunmobi makes an important distinction between 'theatricality' and 'reality'. She provides a neologism, 'technorality', to explain the spectrum of 'realities' which emerge when real life orality is transferred to media (especially video). Adejunmobi explains that 'the growth of local media industries is reshaping how Africans experience reality' (179). She presents a nuanced and copiously referenced explanation of the way in which oral genres (such as Pentacostalist preaching in Nigeria) become theatricalized by having the sermons videoed.

Chapter 10, 'Literary Insurgence in the Kenyan Urban Space', by Miriam Maranga-Musonye, describes an oral form called *Mchongoano*, created within the last two decades by impoverished children from Nairobi's ghettos. Maranga-Musonye relates the form, which consists of ritual insults, to the rise of a hybrid slang called *Sheng*, which is like a Kenyan version of South African *Tsotsitaal*. Through numerous examples Maranga-Musonye meticulously uncovers the various functions of *Mchongoano* in providing the children with a sense of ownership of their localized culture and a weapon of comic resistance to the insults that they are exposed to in everyday life.

In Part IV, Chapter 11, 'Music for Troubled Times' by Innocentia Mhlambi, analyses a jazz song about the forced separation of the song's persona from his wife, Nomalenga. Innocentia provides the words of this jazz classic by Caiphus Semenya, as well as a translation. She contrasts this pathos-soaked Apartheid era number with a rehashed version of the song by South African rap artist, Zuluboy. The situation (enforced separation) is the same, but the latter uses the language of the township youth and carries the same subversive urban attitude as the *Mchongoano* in Nairobi.

Chapter 12, 'Archiving the Present' by Grace Musila, is a densely argued article about Kenyan author Parselelo Kantai. Musila states that she is interested in 'the increasing muddying of the waters that lie in the continuum between popular and canonical arts in recent years' (245). She throws light on a phenomenon facing literature from different parts of Africa: authors' desire to experiment with various combinations of genres, such as autobiography and cartooning, or poetry and sci-fi. This is all part of a willingness to venture into genre writing which in the 1960s and 70s would have been considered unsuitable. Musila also raises the issue of whether the financial support from the Goethe Institute and the Ford Foundation for the series of books, *Kwani?*, initiated by Kantai, is helpful or detrimental. The writing in *Kwani?*, however heterodox, is nearer to the canonical pole of the continuum, while *Mchongoano* is nearer the insurrectionary pole. Musila believes all genres are useful for their roles in 'chronicling of fragments of popular memory in an attempt to counter the culture of collective amnesia'(254). She thus reaffirms what other authors have noted: the importance of popular culture as an archive of the ephemeral.

The last two chapters of Part IV, Popular Discourses of the Streets, along with Chapter 15 in the Coda, remind the reader of the difficulty in drawing a neat circle around African popular culture as the subject of an academic discipline. Peter Simatei's article, '*Heshima Hukuta*: Local-language radio and the performance of Fang culture in Kenya', with its depiction of community radio's importance, is clearly within the tradition of cultural studies, whose origins had strong links to media studies. However, James Tsaaior's article on 'Football as Social Unconscious, or the Cultural Logic of Late Imperialism in Post-Colonial Nigeria' is arguably on the margin between popular culture and anthropology.

Chapter 15, simply entitled 'Coda', is a bizarre contribution. It is a very self-reflective account of how the author, Ranka Primorac, undertook her research on the Zambian author of ChiBemba novels, Stephen Mpashi. I am surprised that Primorac makes no reference to Mpashi's very popular script-writing for radio soap operas in the 1950s. However, since this is clearly a work in progress I cannot really complain. Perhaps this is the editors' way of teasing the reader with the possibility that post-modernist approaches to literature or music can also be applied to *criticism* of those arts.

Inevitably, in a subject as broad as African popular culture, a reviewer will find some gaps. The two media which are under-represented are drama and film/video. The only reason I can imagine for their low profile here is that theatre is a specialization of Karin Barber, while Onookome Okome is an acknowledged expert on the Nollywood film/video industry. Perhaps Okome and Barber feel there is already enough easily accessible literature on these media.

However, this speculation is a minor quibble. *Popular Culture in Africa* is a very welcome addition to the growing literature on the topic. It is particularly gratifying to see so many young academics tackling a huge variety of issues and cultures. It is also gratifying to see that, of the fifteen authors represented in the book, ten are women.

A common motif is the need for more research. I hope that among these research areas some will choose to look at the issue of patronage (using the word very loosely to include any support to artists). It would also be interesting for someone to respond thoroughly to the provocative theories of popular cinema put forward by William Harrow in his book *Trash*. The time is probably right for scholars to look at the issue of religion, not only as a topic but as a social context influencing public reception of popular culture. Finally, the impact of social media on diasporic culture and on ways of evaluating the impact of various digital media on old and emergent art forms needs urgently to be addressed.

REFERENCES

Barber, Karin (1987) 'Popular Arts in Africa', *African Studies Review*, 30 (3): 1-78
—— (1997) 'Views from the Field', in Karin Barber (ed.) *Readings in African Popular Culture* (Bloomington, IN: Indiana University Press), 1-12
Harrow, Kenneth (2013) *Trash: African Cinema from Below* (Bloomington & Indianapolis: Indiana University Press)
Williams, Raymond (1989) *Resources of Hope: Culture, democracy, socialism* (London: Verso) 'Culture is Ordinary', 3-14
—— (2001) 'Base and Superstructure in Marxist Theory', in Meenakshi Durham and Douglas Kellner, *Media and Cultural Studies: Keyworks* (Oxford: Blackwell), 130-143

David Kerr
University of Botswana

Isidore Diala (ed.), *Syncretic Africas: Essays on Postcolonial African Drama and Theatre for Esiaba Irobi*
Amsterdam & New York: Rodopi, 2014. Cross Cultures: vol. 177
ISBN 978042038981, $119. E-book ISBN 97801211802, $106

This is in many ways an excellent volume. Divided into two parts, the first is an homage to, and critique of, the life and work of the protean spirit that was Esiaba Irobi, while the second consists of ten essays on aspects of African theatre in Nigeria, South Africa, Kenya, Eygpt and Uganda.

Part One consists of recollections, poetry and critical writing about Irobi's ouevre, all, I think, by people who knew the man, some for most of his lifetime. The writing by Esiaba's close friends, Olu Oguibe and Georgina Alaukwu-Ehuriah, I found deeply moving. They introduce us to a man in his youth and particularly, at Nsukka University, with huge energy and immense creative and intellectual talent. This Esiaba Irobi has to have his meagre stipend kept for him by his friends because otherwise he spends it all on books and forgets to eat or even clothe himself properly. He reads voraciously, debates furiously; he acts so intensely none can forget his performances: he produces poetry, plays and critical writing. Already the Irobi who rages at perceived injustices, both political and personal, is in full flow, but time after time his friends, Oguibe, Alaukwu-Ehuriah, Martin Banham and Femi Osofisan, speak of the other side of this volcanic man: of his kindness, tenderness, generosity and loyalty. Perhaps Osofisan offers the most succinct description when he speaks of Irobi's 'humanity, his fearlessness, his peppery and polymorphic brilliance' (42).

At Nsukka in the 1980s Irobi demonstrated his towering acting abilities: the more intense the role, the more riveting his performance. None who saw him perform as Elesin Oba in Soyinka's *Death and the King's Horseman* can forget the utter commitment he brought to the part and how he came to embody the ritual tragedy at the heart of this greatest of African plays. During these years he was also prolific. Plays flowed out of him. *The Pope Lied, What Songs Do Mosquitoes Sing, The Colour of Rusting Gold, Nwokedi, The Fronded Circle,* and *Hangmen Also Die* were all written and produced in the 1980s while he was first a student and then a junior lecturer at the University in the heart of the Igbo territory which so inspired his work. Poetry too: his volumes, *Gold, Frankincense and Myrrh* and *Inflorescence* were both published in 1989 just before he left Nigeria.

Isidore Diala and Henry Obi Ajumeze both offer insightful analyses of Irobi's theatre, and many of their views are backed up by the man himself in an interview he gave in 2007 to Leon Osu. They explain how Irobi argued passionately (when did he argue any other way?) for an African aesthetics rooted in orature, mythology, ritual and embodied performance, quite overlooked as he saw it by Western scholarship and analyses of African theatre. This theatre is of course influenced by a well informed knowledge of European theatre traditions, and though, as has always been the case for the Soyinkan theatre he so admired, rooted in his own culture, and often speaking about the Nigerian political world, it is a theatre which he saw as having universal relevance and application.

After increasingly acrimonious disputes with senior colleagues at the University of Nsukka and resentment at being passed over for theatrical and creative writing awards (a trope that sadly recurred throughout his life) Irobi decided that an adverse academic environment, plus the poisonous politics of Nigeria, meant he should head abroad in search of his PhD and a more congenial academic environment. Unfortunately this did not provide the solution he was looking for. Oguibe discusses 'The Tragedy of [Irobi's] Exile', where for the rest of his life, mostly in Britain and then the United States, Irobi was increasingly angry and frustrated. With plays overlooked he gradually stopped seeking to get his theatre published or performed. He said he was turning to academic writing, but relatively little was published. A number of commentators quote Irobi's tragic analysis of his situation on exiting Nigeria: 'I leave to live. I exit to exist.' Sadly this was all too true. Only in his last few years, finally happily married, and finding a more congenial academic environment in Germany, did Esiaba Irobi begin to re-find optimism about writing. On his 2010 death from meningitis, after years of treatment for cancer, his friends found a host of works-in-progress; plays, poetry and critical writing in various stages of completion.

I never met Esiaba Irobi, though I was once the subject of one of his not infrequent vitriolic and vile, widely broadcast emails, when I wrote a review of a book (not one of his) that he felt was unjust. Undoubtedly the loss was mine. Irobi was an exceptional man possessed of a brilliant creative mind, who was driven for many years to rage (largely impotently) across three continents, against a world he found bigoted, prejudiced and corrupt. The second part of *Syncretic Africas* offers essays by many leading commentators on African theatre. Three works on recent South African theatre unknowingly set up a fascinating debate about the performing arts in a post-apartheid nation. Hein Willemse is a professor of Afrikaans, Anton Krueger is a prolific English language theatre academic and playwright, and Bhekizizwe Peterson is professor of African Literature and a theatre activist of many years standing. Willemse in his 'Autobiography as Counter-Memory in *The Orange Earth* of Adam Small' discusses this 'coloured' author who saw himself as essentially Afrikaans but turned to writing his play of rage and revolution in English because of the humiliations visited upon him and his family by Afrikaaner-led apartheid. Anton Krueger discusses a range of post-apartheid plays, bemoaning how much they are infected by South Africa's history of violence, especially male violence. He concludes by making a case for theatre that forgets the past, and forgets issues of national angst and identity. This seems to me a fairly extraordinary position, especially in the light of Peterson's piece on 'The Afrika Cultural Centre'. Peterson discusses the history of this township theatre making and training movement with which he was involved for twenty years, until the recent government focus on theatre as a 'cultural industry' meant funding for such a community initiative could no longer be found. The perspectives from black and white positions remain notably different and significantly at odds with each other. The South African grouping is completed by Temple Hauptfleisch who offers a history of theatre criticism in South Africa and bemoans the lack of contemporary professional critics.

Another interesting and complementary pairing is that of the two articles by Christine Matzke and Oluseyi Ogunjobi, which address different aspects of the theatre of Duro Ladipo. Ladipo offers a number of parallels with Irobi. He too made theatre infused with Nigerian mythology and ritual, and as a performer he also riveted audiences with his embodiment of Sango in his pre-eminent play, *Oba Ko So*; so much so that both he and many of his admirers came to see him as a living incarnation of the god-king he played so often. Ogunjobi gives us a history of the production of the play and many insights into the life and work of Ladipo. Christine Matzke takes the opportunity to interview one of the last of Ladipo's collaborators, the multi-talented Chief Muraina Oyelami, who discusses a life in theatre, art and music. The final article on Nigerian theatre, Kene Igweonu's 'African Drama and the Construction of an Indigenous Cultural Identity: An examination of Four Major Nigerian Plays' is the only really weak contribution. Igweonu continuously conflates Nigeria and Africa and makes statements about the 'essential' nature of African theatre based on just four Nigerian plays, which are by no means representative of the theatre of that nation, let alone the continent.

Christopher Balme raises interesting questions about how imperialism and discourses of modernity influenced the establishment of Egypt's early theatre buildings in his 'Theatre and Modernization in the First Age of Globalization: The Cairo Opera House'. Christopher Odhiambo Joseph offers a useful analysis of two Kenyan plays, Cajetan Boy's *Benta* and John Sibi-Okumu's *Role Play*, both written around the time of the millennium. He focuses on middle class narratives of anxiety, especially as he sees it, refracted through the lens of the treatment of maids. This is a welcome contribution since so little has been written in recent years on Kenyan plays. Finally, I was fascinated by Don Rubin's masterful and brilliantly researched article on Robert Serumaga. Rubin parallels Serumaga with Soyinka but there are also similarities with Irobi. The man's life as experimental dramatist, CIA agent, freedom fighter and lover is surely worthy of major film treatment, but Rubin also makes good claims for Serumaga to be re-assessed as a major African playwright.

I learnt an immense amount from this book, primarily about Esiaba Irobi, but also about many other important, often overlooked playwrights and theatre movements. *Syncretic Africas* is a book which should be on the shelves of any scholar of African theatre, and is a worthy tribute to the man it honours.

Jane Plastow
University of Leeds

Emmanuel Fru Doh, *The Obasinjom Warrior: The life and works of Bate Besong*
Bamenda, Cameroon: Langaa RPCIG, 2014, 230 pp. Distributed by African Books Collective, PO Box 721, Oxford OX1 9EN
ISBN 9789956792016, £18.95.

Emmanuel Fru Doh's book introduces the reader to Bate Besong's poetic and dramatic works and their interpretation at a time when the Cameroonian political landscape is undergoing changes. He begins usefully with Besong's biography and builds a broad historiography, linking some of Besong's life experiences with his literary concerns. The second section is devoted to the published poetry. The final part is a study of six plays: *The Most Cruel Death of the Talkative Zombie* (1986), *Beasts of No Nation* (1990) *Requiem for the Last Kaiser* (1991), *The Banquet* (1994), *Change Waka and His Man Sawa Boy* (2001) and *Once Upon Great Lepers* (2003). Here, in a wide-ranging, although not always articulate, discussion, the author begins to unravel the aesthetic and political potential of Besong's plays from the extensive variety of Cameroonian writing. A close textual analysis of the play texts is presented. Doh captures messages of political resistance against corrupt governments and religious institutions, previously concealed from the reader/audience of the contemporary political and social crises, through the use of culturally specific symbols, and of multiple languages including Afrikaans, Ewodo, Hausa and French. Throughout this part, and within the discussion of the six plays, Doh manages to interface history, drama, politics, religion and issues of freedom, and this enhances the depth of his analysis. The sections on *Requiem for the Last Kaiser* and *Beasts of No Nation* offer strong readings of these plays. The significant space devoted to *Requiem for the Last Kaiser* concentrates on more complex thematic concerns, neo-colonialism and gender, and underlines the playwright's vision expressed at the beginning of the book. Doh aimed to highlight Besong's work as a struggle to expose the corrupt system of governance in anglophone and French Cameroon thus enabling readers to relate his views to other areas of Cameroonian drama and performance.

The section concerned with *The Most Cruel Death of the Talkative Zombie* is particularly interesting. Doh's analysis of the significance of Besong's avant-gardist approach to communicate his message in this play came at a critical point for Cameroon and other West African post-colonial societies and shows the opportunities and understanding to be gained by re-evaluating the pre-colonial political and aesthetic values. The last chapter reiterates the view that European literary and dramatic aesthetics influenced Besong's style (p. 190).

Finally, I would like to note that the book is not carefully edited and there are numerous cases of laxity throughout, which detract from the pleasure of reading.

Sam Kasule
University of Derby

Sergei N. Durylin, *Ira Aldridge* (translated by Alexei Lalo with an essay by Viktoria N. Toropova on Sergei N. Durylin, edited by Bernth Lindfors)

Trenton, NJ: Africa World Press, 2014, 234 pp.
ISBN 9781592219810, $29.95

Interest in the remarkable nineteenth-century African American actor Ira Aldridge seems to be gathering quite some momentum, perhaps stimulated by the recent appearance of the multi-volume biography by Bernth Lindfors, who, perhaps unsurprisingly, crops up as the editor of the book under review. It is a fitting association, as Russian polymath Sergei Durylin turns out to be Lindfors' original predecessor in that he was the first scholar to publish a biography of Aldridge (1940).

Durylin's account concentrates on the Shakespearean performances Aldridge gave in Russia from the late 1850s to mid-1860s, which consisted mainly of his signature role Othello, as well as those of Shylock, Macbeth, Lear and Richard III. Durylin also mentions the role of comic servant Mungo in Isaac Bickerstaffe's *The Padlock*, which Aldridge used not only to demonstrate his complete skills as an actor but also to aid his subversion of audiences' expectations of a black actor.

Trawling through newspaper reports and actors' memoirs, Durylin assembled a lively picture of how Aldridge performed on stage, and how audiences responded to his performances in a country whose theatre-going public loved Shakespeare but had never before seen a black classical actor. Some, although baffled by Aldridge's 'unrestrained' and 'genuinely savage' acting (33), acknowledged that his 'talent is so enormous that it quickly demolishes these routine impressions' (33-4). Most, however, seemed to agree more with the critic who praised Aldridge for his 'simplicity and truthful acting' (34). There were fierce adversaries, and it would have been incredible, says Durylin, if there had not been, given that Russia was a serf empire and Aldridge was showing Europe what a slave could do. He was even banned in St Petersburg. Nevertheless, he liked Russia, which saw him performing at the height of his powers, and, in general the Russians repaid the compliment. Through his research, Durylin looks in detail at Aldridge's portrayal of the major roles in St Petersburg, Moscow and the 'Provinces' and at his relationships with Russian actors, all of which provides rich material about the nature of theatre in Russia at the time.

The early passages, in which Durylin deals with Aldridge's career in North America, England and Germany, rely on poor and often erroneous source material, and have now been overtaken by Lindfors' scholarship. The final pages, contrasting the fate of a black actor forced to flee his homeland and the freedom gained for ethnic theatre in the Soviet Union, must be read as sadly naïve, if well meaning.

Durylin's book, which this edition makes fully available in English for the first time, has been influential in Russian theatre studies and in Aldridge research elsewhere. The pioneering English-language study *Ira Aldridge: The Negro Tragedian* (1958), written by Herbert Marshall (who spoke Russian) and Mildred Stock, draws heavily on Durylin's work for its Russian episodes.

The volume contains an informative essay on Durylin by Viktoria Toropova, a philologist who lives in Moscow, detailing his influence in several fields as a literary and art critic, ethnographer, archaeologist, religious thinker, philosopher and poet. He is recalled primarily as a pioneer of the scholarly discipline of theatre studies in Russia, and this biography of Aldridge was one of the books that helped cement this reputation.

Colin Chambers
Kingston University

Christina S. McMahon, *Recasting Transnationalism Through Performance: Theatre festivals in Cape Verde, Mozambique and Brazil*
Basingstoke & New York: Palgrave Macmillan, Studies in International Performance Series, 2013, ISBN 9781137006806, £55

Christine S. McMahon's book is part of the award-winning series 'Studies in International Performance' and contributes to the timely conversation regarding international theatre festivals, transnationalism and cultural identities. She does this by providing an analysis of African performances from Cape Verde, Angola, Guinea Bissau and Mozambique that challenges fixed narratives of identity and history on a lusophone theatre festival circuit that includes Cape Verde, Brazil and Mozambique in the first decade of the twenty-first century, adding to recent publications on festivals, including Hauptfleisch et al. (2007) *Festivalising! Theatrical Events, Politics and Culture*, and *African Theatre 12: Festivals* (Gibbs, 2013).

'Recasting Transnationalism' is an expansion of McMahon's doctoral project and provides a comprehensive understanding of the author's theoretical research and fieldwork practices. From the outset, McMahon offers an elucidating introduction which presents her main arguments and research questions, and signals awareness of possible controversies her work may induce. She arranges a theoretical framework (referencing the scholarship of Henri Schoenmakers, Richard Paul Knowls, Temple Hauptfleisch and William Sauter) which debates the challenges that globalized theatre venues, such as international festival settings, provoke in relation to community building. She adds to the current discussion by proposing that, due to their smaller scale in relation to other international theatre festivals and a common language attained by their shared colonial past, lusophone transnational theatre festivals are able to promote spaces for dialogue and dissent over artistic showmanship, enabling the possibility of community building and a thought-provoking experience for participants. The author suggests that this subsists through an analysis of the festival's frameworks (theme, performances, workshops, round tables, social gatherings etc.) alongside what she calls 'festival aftermath'.

McMahon studies the concept of Lusofonia in depth in her second chapter, 'Mapping Festivals'. She problematizes common ideologies used to formulate lusophone identity as potential forms of neo-colonialism, defined particularly in these lusophone African countries' relationships with Portugal, and currently with Brazil. However, she also acknowledges that this lusophone community generates opportunities for African artists to challenge fixed notions and narratives related to their countries by performing in these transnational theatre settings. Her analysis presents Lusofonia as a politically flexible discourse and she demonstrates this by mapping the three festivals she addresses and exploring how they negotiate the lusophone ideal: Mindelact in Cape Verde challenges the language hierarchy by staging performances in Creole; Festival d'Agosto in Mozambique tactically resisted officially adopting the term in its rhetoric due to the country's geographical proximity with anglophone nations; and FESTLIP in Brazil, which embraces the ideal as part of a political and economic plan concerning Brazil-Africa relations. Thus, McMahon argues that transnationalism is an 'inherently contentious concept when its major signifier is a common language and that international theatre festivals are productive places for bringing these polemical cultural dialogues to light' (36).

The author's core work offers significant material to the field of performance analysis in relation to transnational festivals' frameworks. The chapters 'Recasting the Colonial Past, African Women on Festival Circuits' and 'Adaptation and the (Trans)Nation' provide exceptional comparative material by examining different angles of lusophone African performances (which address issues of race, colonial histories, gender, language hierarchies and adaptations of Western 'classics') and how they recast these notions by performing in transnational theatre settings. In chapter 5 she illustrates how 'festival aftermath' is an important dimension and must be accounted for when analysing theatre festivals. She exposes the productive space that resonates in the aftermath by analysing how artists can recast and challenge the ideologies behind theatre festivals' processes per se with adaptations of Shakespeare in Cape Verde, and with a successful intercultural adaptation of Cervantes' Don Quixote in Mozambique.

As McMahon expands towards a conclusion, she provides an example of a thriving performance from Guinea Bissau's Theatre of the Oppressed (TO) group that challenged audience perspectives and misconceptions related to African countries' cultures and traditions by using Forum Theatre. She inverts Quetzil Castañeda's terms of 'invisible ethnographers' by proposing that, in international theatre festivals, TO artists may become invisible ethnographers, conducting anthropological inquiries disguised as theatre, and thus gain 'more information about the latent prejudices and gaps in knowledge of audiences than actual solutions to the oppression being depicted in the forum theatre piece' (169).

Throughout her book the author demonstrates how 'recasting trans-nationalism' means reassessing global issues from the perspective of seemingly marginal countries. She suggests that the principal value of Lusofonia may be the productive tensions it generates, and her research focuses on the fundamental interpretative agency of African artists from different former Portuguese colonies to both compare and recast their particular narratives of nationhood, gender and colonialism in these festival venues. McMahon's book is essential reading for those interested in wider African performances, lusophone ideology and performance analysis in relation to transnational theatre festivals, and invites readers to 'recast' their own perspectives related to these conceptions.

Luana Tavano Garcia
University of Warwick

Olakunbi Olasope (ed.), *Black Dionysos: Conversations with Femi Osofisan*
Ibadan: Kraft Books, 2013, 331 pp.
ISBN 9789789181094, n.p

Olakunbi Olasope, those she acknowledges as supporting her and Kraft Books are to be congratulated on recognizing the importance of Femi Osofisan and making his words more widely available. In three sections, headed 'Adaptations', 'Revolutionary Theatre' and 'Writing', *Black Dionysos* brings together fifteen exchanges with Osofisan. These cover 305 pages, and are followed by a few pages of 'snaps', a list of 'select references', an appendix (containing a curriculum vitae), notes on contributors, and an index. At the heart of the book are the exchanges, including some very valuable interviews. These vary in quality and only a few of them are, in the vocabulary of the subtitle, 'conversations'. In that category I place the dialogues with Biodun Jeyifo, which have a particular intimacy, depth, value and intellectual engagement.

Among the most stilted of the exchanges is that with the editor of the volume. Entitled 'Painting a Cross-Cultural Canvas: Osofisan's journey between Athens and Yorubaland', Olakunbi Olasope opened as follows: 'Classicists have identified the convergences between Greek and Nigerian theatres, which have allowed Nigerian playwrights to appropriate Greek tragedy as theirs. And I have been startled to observe the number of ancient issues that are reflected in our world today. It is thus fascinating to compare and contrast ancient and modern approaches to the dissemination of information and knowledge.' After these ponderous words, she 'popped' her question: 'Why, in your own case, do you think that there are numerous similarities between the Greek and Yoruba cultures, mythologies and traditions?'

There is a good deal of preamble here, including a complexity of construction and some redundant terms ('why in your own case'!) Fortunately, Osofisan's reply briskly took the discussion from the barren terrain Olasope was trudging across. He began: 'It is difficult for me to say why. I just note these affinities as you do, with the same astonishment, and exploit them for my own dramaturgical purposes.' He then directed Olasope and her enquiry towards those 'anthropologists' who might be interested in her question and went on to provide some surprising context for the conversation they were having. He referred to 'his' students 'here in China'. This is the sort of revelation that questioners dream of, but Olasope failed to pick up on it. She was, it seems, unaware of the importance of 'placing' interviews geographically and in time. Here, and repeatedly in the volume, Osofisan gave good answers to bad questions and guided the discussion in useful directions. However script-bound, convoluted, pompous or 'hung up' the questions, his answers were valuable; as a result, page after page of the book yields valuable points.

Uncertainties in Olasope's interviewing technique are followed by some curious editorial practices. I have already referred to a reluctance to 'place' the interviews, and this fundamental element is consistently missing and missed. My concerns about the book's construction congregate about the presentation of the material in the academic apparatus at the end. There we find, for example, unhelpful overlaps between the 'select references' and Osofisan's curriculum vitae. As a result some creative writing titles, such as *The Chattering and the Song*, and some critical material, such as Muyiwa Awodiya's *The Drama of Femi Osofisan*, are listed twice. It is hard to reconstruct what has happened to create this duplication.

This is not the only unsatisfactory element in the academic apparatus. Both the notes on contributors and the index are 'flaky'. In the notes, the positions and the research interests of all but one of the 'academic' contributors are spelled out in customary terms and in a certain amount of detail. But when it comes to non-academic contributors, Olasope deemed it acceptable to identify them simply as, for example, 'a freelance journalist' or 'a journalist with *The Nation Newspapers*'. To discriminate between collaborators in this way is lazy, condescending and reprehensible. It is an attitude that Osofisan's own career as a journalist (not fully reflected in the CV included) cries out against. In assessing a public art and in engaging in public exchanges, contributions are made and are welcome from all sides. Osofisan's recognition of the importance of newspapers is clear from his writing for the press and his involvement with, in particular, *The Guardian* (Lagos).

As for the index, it is hard to decide where the flaw lies. Was it in deciding the principles on which the index was compiled? Or was it in the execution? The following are among those not indexed, despite being mentioned in the text: Barber (35), Bullock (278), Ezeigbo (283), and Falana (199). To add to her difficulties (and Olasope must be presumed to be responsible) she unnecessarily 'glossed' some of those mentioned. This exercise, clearly a bridge too far for the compiler, put her on a hiding to nothing, and she exposed her ignorance. The following instances of inadequate pigeon-holing are among the more provocative: Augusto Boal is described merely as 'playwright', as are Ngugi wa Thiong'o, Wole Soyinka and 'Derek Walcot' [*sic* in index]. All are much more versatile than the description suggests. And Ken Saro-Wiwa's achievements cannot be summed up in one word, as 'writer'!

This brings me to the point at which I might have begun: the title of the volume, which, I suggest, speaks of cultural cringe. I will put the spelling of 'Dionysos' aside. In this context, I want simply to make the point that the title *Black Dionysos* whisks readers back into the last century, to that time when, acutely conscious of the European 'gaze', the *mbira* was the 'African piano', *bawo* was 'African chess' and Chaka Zulu was 'the Black Napoleon'. That was the world in which *Black Orpheus* was born – and died.

Osofisan is not a 'Black Dionysos'. In reality if not in chronology, he is a 'born-free'; like all masters of the dramatic arts, he ransacks the past, and hunts where he will. He takes as his right the freedom to raid classical Greece, Elizabethan England and recent Nigerian theatre; he draws inspiration from wherever he wants in order to confront the present. His confidence as a playwright comes through in the patience and honesty of his answers to the sometimes inept questions he was asked in the interviews in this volume. His generosity and his willingness to give a good answer to a bad question mean that, despite its shortcomings, this volume is of enduring value.

James Gibbs

Femi Osofisan & Gbemisola Adeoti (eds), *Playwriting in Nigeria Today (Report on the First Playwrights' Confab)*
Ibadan: Mosuro, 2014, 289 pp.
ISBN 9789783786165 (n.p.)

'We're here to deliberate, to exchange ideas, to exchange experiences, and to relax and learn from one another. So [...] we should expect a lot from this conference, from this Confab, but also we should not expect too much; we should be modest in our expectations' (65). That warning note was struck by Biodun Jeyifo in the course of a gathering of Nigerian playwrights hosted by the Institute of Cultural Studies (ICS) and the Department of Theatre Arts on the campus of the Obafemi Awolowo University at Ile-Ife. It was convened by Femi Osofisan and took place over the weekend of 8-10 March 2013.

The Confab began on the Friday evening with a drama workshop made up of sessions on playwriting, scriptwriting, theatre criticism, media reviews and directing. It continued on the Saturday with welcome addresses and then time devoted to playwriting today, the playwright's experience in the contemporary theatre, the history of local playwriting, and the future of playwriting. It closed on the Sunday morning.

Although the subtitle describes *Playwriting in Nigeria Today* as a 'Report' on the Confab, it is in fact a transcription of virtually every 'formal address', panel speaker's contribution and intervention from the floor. Because playwrights are people who have 'found their voices' and because of the give and take encouraged by the Confab format, there were many exchanges.

In the quotation with which I opened, Jeyifo amended his description of the occasion. It was not a 'conference', not a coming together within a formal structure, nor was it even a fully-fledged 'confabulation' or 'talking together'. It was rather an informal, abbreviated, familiar or colloquial version of the latter: a 'confab'. An occasion, as Jeyifo indicated, for deliberation and exchange, where relaxing together would be expected. The transcriptions in *Playwriting in Nigeria Today* make clear that the event was comfortably Nigerian. By this I mean that the exchange of information and ideas took place against the background of appropriate protocols being duly observed! At Ile-Ife, contributions ran what Ola Rotimi might have called the 'giddy gamut': some truths were told, some hobby horses ridden, some visons shared. Interventions ranged from cold, clear analyses to passionate personal statements, by way of, for example, unapologetic belly-aching.

For the outsider coming to this warm, human occasion through cold print, there is much that was new and reassuring. There were also some things that were surprising, including the expectation that writers would fund productions of their plays! I was also taken aback by the vehemence with which some rejected self-publishing, by the access that some assumed to large casts and by the distance some put between themselves and (their brothers and sisters who were) stand-up performers.

Femi Osofisan, the Grand Motivator of the occasion, contributes an Introduction to the volume in which he writes of anticipating that twenty or thirty might attend the event, only to find that it attracted over a hundred. The list of attendees is a roll-call of those involved in creating and discussing Nigerian theatre during the last half century, including J.P. Clark, Rasheed Gbadamosi, Segun Sofowote, Kalu Uka, Olu Obafemi, Tunde Fatunde, Barclays Ayakoroma, Uko Atai and Jahman Anikulapo. The Introduction also includes a break-down of the themes that struck Osofisan.

The co-editor (and Director of ICS) Gbemisola Adeoti provided a useful Foreword, with a check-list of the main topics covered. He went on to list the publishers represented at the Confab, mentioning Heinemann Books Nigeria, Evans, University Press, Spectrum, Kraft and Mosoro. Although publishers came in for considerable criticism during the Confab, these representatives seem to have bitten their lips, lost their tongues, or felt it was not their place to defend themselves. However, it could be argued that Mosoro had the last word since they have brought out the proceedings as a handsome volume.

Adeoti added a useful historical dimension to his Foreword by suggesting that the gathering at Ife should be linked to the Conference of Theatre Practitioners held in Port Harcourt in 1975. Playwrights certainly need to be kept in touch with 'theatre practitioners', and those setting out 'now' should be aware of what happened 'then'. Nigerian giants, including Hubert Ogunde and Duro Ladipo, were present at the earlier occasion about which, I think, comparatively little has been written and still less remembered. Looking at the profiles of the businesses run by Ogunde and Ladipo, it is apparent that both were astute judges of possibilities for generating cash. Those involved in Nigerian theatre today could benefit from deeper awareness of the experience of such people and from a greater breadth of models from the past. Examples of sustainable play-making in Africa include Ghanaian Concert Parties, often called 'Trios' because the companies were sometimes only three-strong, and the protest theatre that came into being under Apartheid. It produced such classics as *Sizwe Bansi is Dead*: 'a two-hander that fits into a VW Beetle'.

Jeyifo sounded a useful warning note about expectation: the problems facing playwrights were not solved at the Confab, but they were usefully ventilated. The publishing of the proceedings makes possible the continuation of the processes of deliberation, exchange and learning from one another.

James Gibbs

Bernth Lindfors, *Early African Entertainments Abroad*
Madison: University of Wisconsin Press, 2014, 238 pp. + 56 illus.
ISBN 978029930164, $29.95

Bernth Lindfors has reclaimed Ira Aldridge for theatre historians in a monumental three-volume study, and Aldridge has a chapter in this book of historical essays; but the purpose of this volume is to expose the exploitation of black 'performers' (willingly or, more often unwillingly) by their white 'masters'. The focus is on the exhibition of 'freaks', variously interpreted, in sideshows, theatres, halls, circuses etc. It would be compounding a felony to blame Lindfors for his righteous indignation about the blatant racism of those who treated them as cash cows. Even so, I found myself wishing that he could find a way of interpolating a clearer acknowledgment of the dominant mind-set as a product of historical and scientific ignorance. If hierarchy is taken for granted, somebody has to be placed at the bottom, and the common ground of assumption and prejudice is still well trodden. I would be more uncomfortable with a book of essays that treated, *seriatim*, the anti-semitism of John Buchan, 'Sapper', Conan Doyle, G.K.Chesterton, Evelyn Waugh and Graham Greene, but I cannot explain why without detecting inverse racism in myself. The inferiority of the black races was taken for granted by the same people who insisted that a woman's place was in the home. Among them, no doubt, was the mill owner, solicitous for his own wife and daughters, who daily employed working women at his looms. It took a massively destructive war to call that judgment into question. Perhaps it is Lindfors's misfortune to be so repeatedly on the right ethical side.

That is not to deride these historical essays. The shamefulness of racism still defaces the democracies of Britain and America, which are the focus of Lindfors's forensic evidence. During the two days I spent with his book, the rise of UKIP in England and the unpunished police killing of two African-Americans in the USA were prominent in news bulletins. The clear urgency of *Early African Entertainments Abroad* is a direct result of the author's principled stance. His black subjects are, for the most part, victims of their white 'managers'. Ira Aldridge (Chapter 3) and 'Zip', who died at the age of 84 in 1926, are exceptional in this respect. Both P.T. Barnum and Captain O.K. White were Zip's benefactors as well as his show-business beneficiaries. More typical is the sad history of the Hottentot Venus (Chapters 1 and 2). Sartjee Baartman had 'a huge steatopygous bottom' (11) which was put on display in the USA, England and France, where she died in 1815. A plaster cast of her body remained an exhibit in the Musée de l'Homme well into the twentieth century. It is on the English court-case to determine her rightful owner/manager that Lindfors focuses in Chapter 1, rightly seeing it as 'a classic confrontation between heated humanitarianism and cold commerce, between the abolitionist conscience and the entrepreneurial ideal, between love and money' (17). Chapter 2 is a lively exploration of big bottoms in Georgian caricature. There is room for further exploration here. All four of the Anglo-German Georges had steatopygous bottoms, as did Robert Walpole, William IV and Lord Grenville, and scurrilous cartoons, many of them lavatorial, proliferated throughout the long eighteenth century.

By way of Sartjee Baartman, the 'civilized' world's response to the clicking sounds of San speech, and the conjoined twin daughters of a North American slave, Lindfors reasons his way to a troubling conclusion: 'At the very heart of European cultural policy, in Africa and elsewhere, was a supercilious belief in the benevolence of cultural genocide' (85). It is, arguably, a pity that Charles Dickens is singled out by Lindfors's questing searchlight. Compassionate about his starving countrymen, he shared the Victorian insouciance about alien peoples. In a misjudged attempt at humour, Dickens committed to the permanence of print a full-throated rejection of the idea of the 'noble savage': 'I call a savage a something highly desirable to be civilised off the face of the earth' (97). We Europeans are not easily excused.

Peter Thomson
University of Exeter

Books Received and Noted

Full reviews will be carried in AT15.

Alain Ricard, *Wole Soyinka et Nestor Zinsou: De la scene a l'espace public.* Paris: Editions Karthala. ISBN 9782811113810 (pbk).€19.00

Hakeem Bello, *The Interpreters: Ritual, Violence and Social Regeneration in the Writing of Wole Soyinka.* Ibadan: Kraft Books. ISBN 9789789181957 (pbk). £6 (available from African Book Collective, PO Box 721, Oxford OX1 9EN)

Isidore Diala, *Esiaba Irobi's Drama and the Postcolony*. Ibadan: Kraft Books. ISBN 9789789181131 (pbk). £6 (available from African Book Collective, PO Box 721, Oxford OX1 9EN)

Plays published by Kraft Books, Nigeria, are now available through African Book Collective, PO Box 721, Oxford OX1 9EN. In a list circulated in April 2015 ABC offer seven plays published and performed over the last decades. The prolific Ahmed Yerima, sometime Artistic Director of the National Troupe of Nigeria, is represented by three plays: *Orisa Ibeji, Heart of Stone* and *Otaelo* (based on Shakespeare's *Othello*). Other plays listed are *Iredi War* by Sam Ukala, *Maybe Tomorrow* by Seji Cole, and *The State Visit* by Niyi Osundare. Osundare is, of course, renowned as one of Africa's leading poets, but this vigorous political satire, first performed at the University of Ibadan in 1997, and described as 'a manifesto for discourse and action', shows him to be a powerful and engaging playwright.

MB

Lightning Source UK Ltd.
Milton Keynes UK
UKOW04f0037230816

281232UK00014B/439/P